Cambridge Elements

Elements in Quantitative Finance
edited by
Riccardo Rebonato
EDHEC Business School

MACHINE LEARNING FOR ASSET MANAGERS

Marcos M. López de Prado
Cornell University

CAMBRIDGE
UNIVERSITY PRESS

CAMBRIDGE
UNIVERSITY PRESS

University Printing House, Cambridge CB2 8BS, United Kingdom

One Liberty Plaza, 20th Floor, New York, NY 10006, USA

477 Williamstown Road, Port Melbourne, VIC 3207, Australia

314–321, 3rd Floor, Plot 3, Splendor Forum, Jasola District Centre, New Delhi – 110025, India

79 Anson Road, #06–04/06, Singapore 079906

Cambridge University Press is part of the University of Cambridge.

It furthers the University's mission by disseminating knowledge in the pursuit of education, learning, and research at the highest international levels of excellence.

www.cambridge.org
Information on this title: www.cambridge.org/9781108792899
DOI: 10.1017/9781108883658

First published 2020

A catalogue record for this publication is available from the British Library.

ISBN 978-1-108-79289-9 Paperback
ISSN 2631-8571 (online)
ISSN 2631-8563 (print)

Machine Learning for Asset Managers

Elements In Quantitative Finance

DOI: 10.1017/9781108883658
First published online: April 2020

Marcos M. López de Prado
Cornell University
Author for correspondence: ml863@cornell.edu

Abstract: Successful investment strategies are specific implementations of general theories. An investment strategy that lacks a theoretical justification is likely to be false. Hence, an asset manager should concentrate her efforts on developing a theory rather than on backtesting potential trading rules. The purpose of this Element is to introduce machine learning (ML) tools that can help asset managers discover economic and financial theories. ML is not a black box, and it does not necessarily overfit. ML tools complement rather than replace the classical statistical methods. Some of ML's strengths include: (1) a focus on out-of-sample predictability instead of in-sample variance adjudication; (2) the use of computational methods to avoid relying on (potentially unrealistic) assumptions; (3) the ability to "learn" complex specifications, including nonlinear, hierarchical, and noncontinuous interaction effects in a high-dimensional space; and (4) the ability to disentangle the variable search from the specification search, in a manner that is robust to multicollinearity and other substitution effects.

Keywords: machine learning, unsupervised learning, supervised learning, clustering, classification, labeling, portfolio construction

JEL classifications: G0, G1, G2, G15, G24, E44
AMS classifications: 91G10, 91G60, 91G70, 62C, 60E

ISBNs: 9781108792899 (PB), 9781108883658 (OC)
ISSNs: 2631-8571 (online), 2631-8563 (print)

Contents

1 Introduction

1.1 Motivation

To a greater extent than other mathematical disciplines, statistics is a product of its time. If Francis Galton, Karl Pearson, Ronald Fisher, and Jerzy Neyman had had access to computers, they may have created an entirely different field. Classical statistics relies on simplistic assumptions (linearity, independence), in-sample analysis, analytical solutions, and asymptotic properties partly because its founders had access to limited computing power. Today, many of these legacy methods continue to be taught at university courses and in professional certification programs, even though computational methods, such as cross-validation, ensemble estimators, regularization, bootstrapping, and Monte Carlo, deliver demonstrably better solutions. In the words of Efron and Hastie (2016, 53),

> two words explain the classic preference for parametric models: mathematical tractability. In a world of sliderules and slow mechanical arithmetic, mathematical formulation, by necessity, becomes the computational tool of choice. Our new computation-rich environment has unplugged the mathematical bottleneck, giving us a more realistic, flexible, and far-reaching body of statistical techniques.

Financial problems pose a particular challenge to those legacy methods, because economic systems exhibit a degree of complexity that is beyond the grasp of classical statistical tools (López de Prado 2019b). As a consequence, machine learning (ML) plays an increasingly important role in finance. Only a few years ago, it was rare to find ML applications outside short-term price prediction, trade execution, and setting of credit ratings. Today, it is hard to find a use case where ML is not being deployed in some form. This trend is unlikely to change, as larger data sets, greater computing power, and more efficient algorithms all conspire to unleash a golden age of financial ML. The ML revolution creates opportunities for dynamic firms and challenges for antiquated asset managers. Firms that resist this revolution will likely share Kodak's fate. One motivation of this Element is to demonstrate how modern statistical tools help address many of the deficiencies of classical techniques in the context of asset management.

Most ML algorithms were originally devised for cross-sectional data sets. This limits their direct applicability to financial problems, where modeling the time series properties of data sets is essential. My previous book, *Advances in Financial Machine Learning* (AFML; López de Prado 2018a), addressed the challenge of modeling the time series properties of financial data sets with ML algorithms, from the perspective of an academic who also happens to be a practitioner.

Machine Learning for Asset Managers is concerned with answering a different challenge: how can we use ML to build better financial theories? This is not a philosophical or rhetorical question. Whatever edge you aspire to gain in finance, it can only be justified in terms of someone else making a systematic mistake from which you benefit.[1] Without a testable theory that explains your edge, the odds are that you do not have an edge at all. A historical simulation of an investment strategy's performance (backtest) is not a theory; it is a (likely unrealistic) simulation of a past that never happened (you did not deploy that strategy years ago; that is why you are backtesting it!). Only a theory can pin down the clear cause–effect mechanism that allows you to extract profits against the collective wisdom of the crowds – a testable theory that explains factual evidence as well as counterfactual cases (x implies y, and the absence of y implies the absence of x). Asset managers should focus their efforts on researching theories, not backtesting trading rules. ML is a powerful tool for building financial theories, and the main goal of this Element is to introduce you to essential techniques that you will need in your endeavor.

1.2 Theory Matters

A black swan is typically defined as an extreme event that has not been observed before. Someone once told me that quantitative investment strategies are useless. Puzzled, I asked why. He replied, "Because the future is filled with black swans, and since historical data sets by definition cannot contain never-seen-before events, ML algorithms cannot be trained to predict them." I counterargued that, in many cases, black swans have been predicted.

Let me explain this apparent paradox with an anecdote. Back in the year 2010, I was head of high-frequency futures at a large US hedge fund. On May 6, we were running our liquidity provision algorithms as usual, when around 12:30 ET, many of them started to flatten their positions automatically. We did not interfere or override the systems, so within minutes, our market exposure became very small. This system behavior had never happened to us before. My team and I were conducting a forensic analysis of what had caused the systems to shut themselves down when, at around 14:30 ET, we saw the S&P 500 plunge, within minutes, almost 10% relative to the open. Shortly after, the systems started to buy aggressively, profiting from a 5% rally into the market close. The press dubbed this black swan the "flash crash." We were twice surprised by this episode: first, we could not understand how our systems

---

[1] This is also true in the context of factor investing, where the systematic mistake can be explained in terms of behavioral bias, mismatched investment horizons, risk tolerance, regulatory constraints, and other variables informing investors' decisions.

predicted an event that we, the developers, did not anticipate; second, we could not understand why our systems started to buy shortly after the market bottomed.

About five months later, an official investigation found that the crash was likely caused by an order to sell 75,000 E-mini S&P 500 futures contracts at a high participation rate (CFTC 2010). That large order contributed to a persistent imbalance in the order flow, making it very difficult for market makers to flip their inventory without incurring losses. This toxic order flow triggered stop-out limits across market makers, who ceased to provide liquidity. Market makers became aggressive liquidity takers, and without anyone remaining on the bid, the market inevitably collapsed (Easley et al. 2011).

We could not have forecasted the flash crash by watching CNBC or reading the *Wall Street Journal*. To most observers, the flash crash was indeed an unpredictable black swan. However, the underlying causes of the flash crash are very common. Order flow is almost never perfectly balanced. In fact, imbalanced order flow is the norm, with various degrees of persistency (e.g., measured in terms of serial correlation). Our systems had been trained to reduce positions under extreme conditions of order flow imbalance. In doing so, they were trained to avoid the conditions that shortly after caused the black swan. Once the market collapsed, our systems recognized that the opportunity to buy at a 10% discount offset previous concerns from extreme order flow imbalance, and they took long positions until the close. This experience illustrates the two most important lessons contained in this Element.

1.2.1 Lesson 1: You Need a Theory

Contrary to popular belief, backtesting is not a research tool. Backtests can never prove that a strategy is a true positive, and they may only provide evidence that a strategy is a false positive. Never develop a strategy solely through backtests. Strategies must be supported by theory, not historical simulations. Your theories must be general enough to explain particular cases, even if those cases are black swans. The existence of black holes was predicted by the theory of general relativity more than five decades before the first black hole was observed. In the above story, our market microstructure theory (which later on became known as the VPIN theory; see Easley et al. 2011b) helped us predict and profit from a black swan. Not only that, but our theoretical work also contributed to the market's bounce back (my colleagues used to joke that we helped put the "flash" into the "flash crash"). This Element contains some of the tools you need to discover your own theories.

1.2.2 Lesson 2: ML Helps Discover Theories

Consider the following approach to discovering new financial theories. First, you apply ML tools to uncover the hidden variables involved in a complex phenomenon. These are the ingredients that the theory must incorporate in order to make successful forecasts. The ML tools have identified these ingredients; however, they do not directly inform you about the exact equation that binds the ingredients together. Second, we formulate a theory that connects these ingredients through a structural statement. This structural statement is essentially a system of equations that hypothesizes a particular cause–effect mechanism. Third, the theory has a wide range of testable implications that go beyond the observations predicted by the ML tools in the first step.[2] A successful theory will predict events out-of-sample. Moreover, it will explain not only positives (x causes y) but also negatives (the absence of y is due to the absence of x).

In the above discovery process, ML plays the key role of decoupling the search for variables from the search for specification. Economic theories are often criticized for being based on "facts with unknown truth value" (Romer 2016) and "generally phony" assumptions (Solow 2010). Considering the complexity of modern financial systems, it is unlikely that a researcher will be able to uncover the ingredients of a theory by visual inspection of the data or by running a few regressions. Classical statistical methods do not allow this decoupling of the two searches.

Once the theory has been tested, it stands on its own feet. In this way, the theory, not the ML algorithm, makes the predictions. In the above anecdote, the theory, not an online forecast produced by an autonomous ML algorithm, shut the position down. The forecast was theoretically sound, and it was not based on some undefined pattern. It is true that the theory could not have been discovered without the help of ML techniques, but once the theory was discovered, the ML algorithm played no role in the decision to close the positions two hours prior to the flash crash. The most insightful use of ML in finance is for discovering theories. You may use ML successfully for making financial forecasts; however, that is not necessarily the best scientific use of this technology (particularly if your goal is to develop high-capacity investment strategies).

1.3 How Scientists Use ML

An ML algorithm learns complex patterns in a high-dimensional space with little human guidance on model specification. That ML models need not be specified by the researcher has led many to, erroneously, conclude that ML must

---

[2] A theory can be tested with more powerful tools than backtests. For instance, we could investigate which market makers lost money during the flash crash. Did they monitor for order flow imbalance? Did market makers that monitor for order flow imbalance fare better? Can we find evidence of their earlier retreat in the FIX messages of that day? A historical simulation of a trading rule cannot give us this level of insight.

be a black box. In that view, ML is merely an "oracle,"[3] a prediction machine from which no understanding can be extracted. The black box view of ML is a misconception. It is fueled by popular industrial applications of ML, where the search for better predictions outweighs the need for theoretical understanding. A review of recent scientific breakthroughs reveals radically different uses of ML in science, including the following:

1 **Existence:** ML has been deployed to evaluate the plausibility of a theory across all scientific fields, even beyond the empirical sciences. Notably, ML algorithms have helped make mathematical discoveries. ML algorithms cannot prove a theorem, however they can point to the existence of an undiscovered theorem, which can then be conjectured and eventually proved. In other words, if something can be predicted, there is hope that a mechanism can be uncovered (Gryak et al., forthcoming).

2 **Importance:** ML algorithms can determine the relative informational content of explanatory variables (features, in ML parlance) for explanatory and/ or predictive purposes (Liu 2004). For example, the mean-decrease accuracy (MDA) method follows these steps: (1) Fit a ML algorithm on a particular data set; (2) derive the out-of-sample cross-validated accuracy; (3) repeat step (2) after shuffling the time series of individual features or combinations of features; (4) compute the decay in accuracy between (2) and (3). Shuffling the time series of an important feature will cause a significant decay in accuracy. Thus, although MDA does not uncover the underlying mechanism, it discovers the variables that should be part of the theory.

3 **Causation:** ML algorithms are often utilized to evaluate causal inference following these steps: (1) Fit a ML algorithm on historical data to predict outcomes, absent of an effect. This model is nontheoretical, and it is purely driven by data (like an oracle); (2) collect observations of outcomes under the presence of the effect; (3) use the ML algorithm fit in (1) to predict the observation collected in (2). The prediction error can be largely attributed to the effect, and a theory of causation can be proposed (Varian 2014; Athey 2015).

4 **Reductionist:** ML techniques are essential for the visualization of large, high-dimensional, complex data sets. For example, manifold learning algorithms can cluster a large number of observations into a reduced subset of peer groups, whose differentiating properties can then be analyzed (Schlecht et al. 2008).

---

[3] Here we use a common definition of oracle in complexity theory: a black box that is able to produce a solution for any instance of a given computational problem.

5 **Retriever:** ML is used to scan through big data in search of patterns that humans failed to recognize. For instance, every night ML algorithms are fed millions of images in search of supernovae. Once they find one image with a high probability of containing a supernova, expensive telescopes can be pointed to a particular region in the universe, where humans will scrutinize the data (Lochner et al. 2016). A second example is outlier detection. Finding outliers is a prediction problem rather than an explanation problem. A ML algorithm can detect an anomalous observation, based on the complex structure it has found in the data, even if that structure is not explained to us (Hodge and Austin 2004).

Rather than replacing theories, ML plays the critical role of helping scientists form theories based on rich empirical evidence. Likewise, ML opens the opportunity for economists to apply powerful data science tools toward the development of sound theories.

1.4 Two Types of Overfitting

The dark side of ML's flexibility is that, in inexperienced hands, these algorithms can easily overfit the data. The primary symptom of overfitting is a divergence between a model's in-sample and out-of-sample performance (known as the generalization error). We can distinguish between two types of overfitting: the overfitting that occurs on the train set, and the overfitting that occurs on the test set. Figure 1.1 summarizes how ML deals with both kinds of overfitting.

1.4.1 Train Set Overfitting

Train set overfitting results from choosing a specification that is so flexible that it explains not only the signal, but also the noise. The problem with confounding signal with noise is that noise is, by definition, unpredictable. An overfit model will produce wrong predictions with an unwarranted confidence, which in turn will lead to poor performance out-of-sample (or even in a pseudo-out-of-sample, like in a backtest).

ML researchers are keenly aware of this problem, which they address in three complementary ways. The first approach to correct for train set overfitting is evaluating the generalization error, through resampling techniques (such as cross-validation) and Monte Carlo methods. Appendix A describes these techniques and methods in greater detail. The second approach to reduce train set overfitting is regularization methods, which prevent model complexity unless it can be justified in terms of greater explanatory power. Model

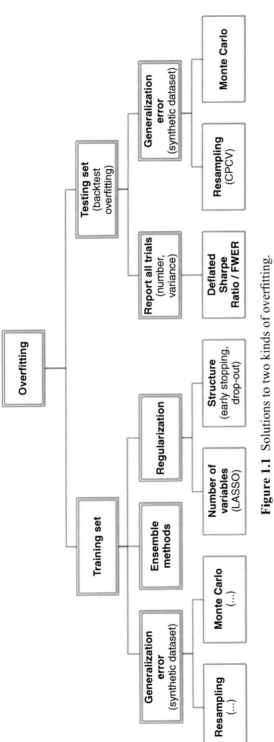

Figure 1.1 Solutions to two kinds of overfitting.

parsimony can be enforced by limiting the number of parameters (e.g., LASSO) or restricting the model's structure (e.g., early stopping). The third approach to address train set overfitting is ensemble techniques, which reduce the variance of the error by combining the forecasts of a collection of estimators. For example, we can control the risk of overfitting a random forest on a train set in at least three ways: (1) cross-validating the forecasts; (2) limiting the depth of each tree; and (3) adding more trees.

In summary, a backtest may hint at the occurrence of train set overfitting, which can be remedied using the above approaches. Unfortunately, backtests are powerless against the second type of overfitting, as explained next.

1.4.2 Test Set Overfitting

Imagine that a friend claims to have a technique to predict the winning ticket at the next lottery. His technique is not exact, so he must buy more than one ticket. Of course, if he buys all of the tickets, it is no surprise that he will win. How many tickets would you allow him to buy before concluding that his method is useless? To evaluate the accuracy of his technique, you should adjust for the fact that he has bought multiple tickets. Likewise, researchers running multiple statistical tests on the same data set are more likely to make a false discovery. By applying the same test on the same data set multiple times, it is guaranteed that eventually a researcher will make a false discovery. This selection bias comes from fitting the model to perform well on the test set, not the train set.

Another example of test set overfitting occurs when a researcher backtests a strategy and she tweaks it until the output achieves a target performance. That backtest–tweak–backtest cycle is a futile exercise that will inevitably end with an overfit strategy (a false positive). Instead, the researcher should have spent her time investigating how the research process misled her into backtesting a false strategy. In other words, a poorly performing backtest is an opportunity to fix the research process, not an opportunity to fix a particular investment strategy.

Most published discoveries in finance are likely false, due to test set over-fitting. ML did not cause the current crisis in financial research (Harvey et al. 2016). That crisis was caused by the widespread misuse of classical statistical methods in finance, and *p-hacking* in particular. ML can help deal with the problem of test set overfitting, in three ways. First, we can keep track of how many independent tests a researcher has run, to evaluate the probability that at least one of the outcomes is a false discovery (known as familywise error rate, or FWER). The deflated Sharpe ratio (Bailey and López de Prado 2014) follows a similar approach in the context of backtesting, as explained in Section 8. It is the equivalent to controlling for the number of lottery tickets that your friend bought. Second, while it is easy to overfit a model to one test set, it is hard to overfit a model to thousands of test sets for each security. Those thousands of test sets can be generated by resampling combinatorial splits of train and test sets. This is the approached followed by the combinatorial purged cross-validation method, or CPCV (AFML, chapter 12). Third, we can use historical series to estimate the underlying data-generating process, and sample synthetic data sets that match the statistical properties observed in history. Monte Carlo methods are particularly powerful at producing synthetic data sets that match the statistical properties of a historical series. The conclusions from these tests are conditional to the representativeness of the estimated data-generating process (AFML, chapter 13). The main advantage of this approach is that those conclusions are not connected to a particular (observed) realization of the data-generating process but to an entire distribution of random realizations. Following with our example, this is equivalent to replicating the lottery game and repeating it many times, so that we can rule luck out.

In summary, there are multiple practical solutions to the problem of train set and test set overfitting. These solutions are neither infallible nor incompatible, and my advice is that you apply all of them. At the same time, I must insist that no backtest can replace a theory, for at least two reasons: (1) backtests cannot simulate black swans – only theories have the breadth and depth needed to consider the never-before-seen occurrences; (2) backtests may insinuate that a strategy is profitable, but they do not tell us why. They are not a controlled experiment. Only a theory can state the cause–effect mechanism, and formulate a wide range of predictions and implications that can be independently tested for facts and counterfacts. Some of these implications may even be testable outside the realm of investing. For example, the VPIN theory predicted that market makers would suffer stop-outs under persistent order flow imbalance. Beyond testing whether order flow imbalance causes a reduction in liquidity, researchers can also test whether market makers suffered losses during the flash crash (hint: they did). This latter test can be conducted by reviewing financial statements, independently from the evidence contained in exchange records of prices and quotes.

1.5 Outline

This Element offers asset managers a step-by-step guide to building financial theories with the help of ML methods. To that objective, each section uses what we have learned in the previous ones. Each section (except for this introduction) contains an empirical analysis, where the methods explained are put to the test in Monte Carlo experiments.

The first step in building a theory is to collect data that illustrate how some variables relate to each other. In financial settings, those data often take the form of a covariance matrix. We use covariance matrices to run regressions, optimize portfolios, manage risks, search for linkages, etc. However, financial covariance matrices are notoriously noisy. A relatively small percentage of the information they contain is signal, which is systematically suppressed by arbitrage forces. Section 2 explains how to denoise a covariance matrix without giving up the little signal it contains. Most of the discussion centers on random matrix theory, but at the core of the solution sits an ML technique: the kernel density estimator.

Many research questions involve the notion of similarity or distance. For example, we may be interested in understanding how *closely* related two variables are. Denoised covariance matrices can be very useful for deriving distance metrics from linear relationships. Modeling nonlinear relationships requires more advanced concepts. Section 3 provides an information-theoretic framework for extracting complex signals from noisy data. In particular, it allows us to define distance metrics with minimal assumptions regarding the underlying variables that characterize the metric space. These distance metrics can be thought of as a nonlinear generalization of the notion of correlation.

One of the applications of distance matrices is to study whether some variables are more closely related among themselves than to the rest, hence forming clusters. Clustering has a wide range of applications across finance, like in asset class taxonomy, portfolio construction, dimensionality reduction, or modeling networks of agents. A general problem in clustering is finding the optimal number of clusters. Section 4 introduces the ONC algorithm, which provides a general solution to this problem. Various use cases for this algorithm are presented throughout this Element.

Clustering is an unsupervised learning problem. Before we can delve into supervised learning problems, we need to assess ways of labeling financial data. The effectiveness of a supervised ML algorithm greatly depends on the kind of problem we attempt to solve. For example, it may be harder to forecast tomorrow's S&P 500 return than the sign of its next 5% move. Different features are appropriate for different types of labels. Researchers should consider carefully what labeling method they apply on their data. Section 5 discusses the merits of various alternatives.

AFML warned readers that backtesting is not a research tool. Feature importance is. A backtest cannot help us develop an economic or financial theory.

In order to do that, we need a deeper understanding of what variables are involved in a phenomenon. Section 6 studies ML tools for evaluating the importance of explanatory variables, and explains how these tools defeat many of the caveats of classical methods, such as the *p*-value. A particular concern is how to overcome *p*-value's lack of robustness under multicollinearity. To tackle this problem, we must apply what we learned in all prior sections, including denoising (Section 2), distance metrics (Section 3), clustering (Section 4), and labeling (Section 5).

Once you have a financial theory, you can use your discovery to develop an investment strategy. Designing that strategy will require making some investment decisions under uncertainty. To that purpose, mean-variance portfolio optimization methods are universally known and used, even though they are notorious for their instability. Historically, this instability has been addressed in a number of ways, such as introducing strong constraints, adding priors, shrinking the covariance matrix, and other robust optimization techniques. Many asset managers are familiar with instability caused by noise in the covariance matrix. Fewer asset managers realize that certain data structures (types of signal) are also a source of instability for mean-variance solutions. Section 7 explains why signal can be a source of instability, and how ML methods can help correct it.

Finally, a financial ML book would not be complete without a detailed treatment of how to evaluate the probability that your discovery is false, as a result of test set overfitting. Section 8 explains the dangers of backtest overfitting, and provides several practical solutions to the problem of selection bias under multiple testing.

1.6 Audience

If, like most asset managers, you routinely compute covariance matrices, use correlations, search for low-dimensional representations of high-dimensional spaces, build predictive models, compute *p*-values, solve mean-variance optimizations, or apply the same test multiple times on a given data set, you need to read this Element. In it, you will learn that financial covariance matrices are noisy and that they need to be cleaned before running regressions or computing optimal portfolios (Section 2). You will learn that correlations measure a very narrow definition of codependency and that various information-theoretic metrics are more insightful (Section 3). You will learn intuitive ways of reducing the dimensionality of a space, which do not involve a change of basis. Unlike PCA, ML-based dimensionality reduction methods provide intuitive results (Section 4). Rather than aiming for implausible fixed-horizon predictions, you will learn alternative ways of posing financial prediction problems that can be solved with higher accuracy (Section 5). You will learn modern alternatives to the classical *p*-values (Section 6). You will learn how to address the instability problem that plagues mean-variance investment portfolios (Section 7). And you will learn how to evaluate the probability that your discovery is false as a result of multiple testing (Section 8). If you work in the asset management industry or in academic finance, this Element is for you.

1.7 Five Popular Misconceptions about Financial ML

Financial ML is a new technology. As it is often the case with new technologies, its introduction has inspired a number of misconceptions. Below is a selection of the most popular.

1.7.1 ML Is the Holy Grail versus ML Is Useless

The amount of hype and counterhype surrounding ML defies logic. Hype creates a set of expectations that may not be fulfilled for the foreseeable future. Counterhype attempts to convince audiences that there is nothing special about ML and that classical statistical methods already produce the results that ML-enthusiasts claim.

ML critics sometimes argue that "caveat X in linear regression is no big deal," where X can either mean model misspecification, multicollinearity, missing regressors, nonlinear interaction effects, etc. In reality, any of these violations of classical assumptions will lead to accepting uninformed variables (a false positive) and/or rejecting informative variables (a false negative). For an example, see Section 6.

Another common error is to believe that the central limit theorem somehow justifies the use of linear regression models everywhere. The argument goes like this: with enough observations, Normality prevails, and linear models provide a good fit to the asymptotic correlation structure. This "CLT Hail Mary pass" is an undergrad fantasy: yes, the *sample mean* converges in distribution to a Gaussian, but not the sample itself! And that converge only occurs if the observations are independent and identically distributed. It takes a few lines of code to demonstrate that a misspecified regression will perform poorly, whether we feed it thousands or billions of observations.

Both extremes (hype and counterhype) prevent investors from recognizing the real and differentiated value that ML delivers today. ML is modern statistics, and it helps overcome many of the caveats of classical techniques that have preoccupied asset managers for decades. See López de Prado (2019c) for multiple examples of current applications of ML in finance.

1.7.2 ML Is a Black Box

This is perhaps the most widespread myth surrounding ML. Every research laboratory in the world uses ML to some extent, so clearly ML is compatible with the scientific method. Not only is ML not a black box, but as Section 6 explains, ML-based research tools can be more insightful than traditional statistical methods (including econometrics). ML models can be interpreted through a number of procedures, such as PDP, ICE, ALE, Friedman's H-stat, MDI, MDA, global surrogate, LIME, and Shapley values, among others. See Molnar (2019) for a detailed treatment of ML interpretability.

Whether someone applies ML as a black box or as a white-box is a matter of personal choice. The same is true of many other technical subjects. I personally do not care much about how my car works, and I must confess that I have never lifted the hood to take a peek at the engine (my thing is math, not mechanics). So, my car remains a black box to me. I do not blame the engineers who designed my car for my lack of curiosity, and I am aware that the mechanics who work at my garage see my car as a white box. Likewise, the assertion that ML is a black box reveals how some people have chosen to apply ML, and it is not a universal truth.

1.7.3 Finance Has Insufficient Data for ML

It is true that a few ML algorithms, particularly in the context of price prediction, require a lot of data. That is why a researcher must choose the right algorithm for a particular job. On the other hand, ML critics who wield this argument seem to ignore that many ML applications in finance do not require any historical data at all. Examples include risk analysis, portfolio construction, outlier detection, feature importance, and bet-sizing methods. Each section in this Element demonstrates the mathematical properties of ML without relying on any historical series. For instance, Section 7 evaluates the accuracy of an ML-based portfolio construction algorithm via Monte Carlo experiments. Conclusions drawn from millions of Monte Carlo simulations teach us something about the general mathematical properties of a particular approach. The anecdotal evidence derived from a handful of historical simulations is no match to evaluating a wide range of scenarios.

Other financial ML applications, like sentiment analysis, deep hedging, credit ratings, execution, and private commercial data sets, enjoy an abundance of data. Finally, in some settings, researchers can conduct randomized controlled experiments, where they can generate their own data and establish precise cause–effect mechanisms. For example, we may reword a news article and compare ML's sentiment extraction with a human's conclusion, controlling for various changes. Likewise, we may experiment with the market's reaction to alternative implementations of an execution algorithm under comparable conditions.

1.7.4 The Signal-to-Noise Ratio Is Too Low in Finance

There is no question that financial data sets exhibit lower signal-to-noise ratio than those used by other ML applications (a point that we will demonstrate in Section 2). Because the signal-to-noise ratio is so low in finance, data alone are not good enough for relying on black box predictions. That does not mean that ML cannot be used in finance. It means that we must use ML differently, hence the notion of financial ML as a distinct subject of study. Financial ML is not the mere application of standard ML to financial data sets. Financial ML comprises ML techniques specially designed to tackle the specific challenges faced by financial researchers, just as econometrics is not merely the application of standard statistical techniques to economic data sets.

The goal of financial ML ought to be to assist researchers in the discovery of new economic theories. The theories so discovered, and not the ML algorithms, will produce forecasts. This is no different than the way scientists utilize ML across all fields of research.

1.7.5 The Risk of Overfitting Is Too High in Finance

Section 1.4 debunked this myth. In knowledgeable hands, ML algorithms overfit less than classical methods. I concede, however, that in nonexpert hands ML algorithms can cause more harm than good.

1.8 The Future of Financial Research

The International Data Corporation has estimated that 80% of all available data are unstructured (IDC 2014). Many of the new data sets available to researchers are high-dimensional, sparse, or nonnumeric. As a result of the complexities of these new data sets, there is a limit to how much researchers can learn using regression models and other linear algebraic or geometric approaches. Even with older data sets, traditional quantitative techniques may fail to capture potentially complex (e.g., nonlinear and interactive) associations among variables, and these techniques are extremely sensitive to the multicollinearity problem that pervades financial data sets (López de Prado 2019b).

Economics and finance have much to benefit from the adoption of ML methods. As of November 26, 2018, the Web of Science[4] lists 13,772 journal

---

[4] www.webofknowledge.com.

articles on subjects in the intersection of "Economics" and "Statistics & Probability." Among those publications, only eighty-nine articles (0.65%) contain any of the following terms: classifier, clustering, neural network, or machine learning. To put it in perspective, out of the 40,283 articles in the intersection of "Biology" and "Statistics & Probability," a total of 4,049 (10.05%) contained any of those terms, and out of the 4,994 articles in the intersection of "Chemistry, Analytical" and "Statistics & Probability," a total of 766 (15.34%) contained any of those terms.

The econometric canon predates the dawn of digital computing. Most econometric models were devised for estimation by hand and are a product of their time. In the words of Robert Tibshirani, "people use certain methods because that is how it all started and that's what they are used to. It's hard to change it."[5] Students in the twenty-first century should not be overexposed to legacy technologies. Moreover, the most successful quantitative investment firms in history rely primarily on ML, not econometrics, and the current predominance of econometrics in graduate studies prepares students for academic careers, not for jobs in the industry.

This does not mean that econometrics has outlived its usability. Researchers asked to decide between econometrics and ML are presented with a false choice. ML and econometrics complement each other, because they have different strengths. For example, ML can be particularly helpful at suggesting to researchers the ingredients of a theory (see Section 6), and econometrics can be useful at testing a theory that is well grounded on empirical observation. In fact, sometimes we may want to apply both paradigms at the same time, like in semiparametric methods. For example, a regression could combine observable explanatory variables with control variables that are contributed by an ML algorithm (Mullainathan and Spiess 2017). Such approach would address the bias associated with omitted regressors (Clarke 2005).

1.9 Frequently Asked Questions

Over the past few years, attendees at seminars have asked me all sorts of interesting questions. In this section I have tried to provide a short answer to some of the most common questions. I have also added a couple of questions that I am still hoping that someone will ask one day.

In Simple Terms, What Is ML?

Broadly speaking, ML refers to the set of algorithms that learn complex patterns in a high-dimensional space without being specifically directed. Let us break

---

[5] https://qz.com/1206229/this-is-the-best-book-for-learning-modern-statistics-its-free/.

that definition into its three components. First, ML learns without being specifically directed, because researchers impose very little structure on the data. Instead, the algorithm derives that structure from the data. Second, ML learns complex patterns, because the structure identified by the algorithm may not be representable as a finite set of equations. Third, ML learns in a high-dimensional space, because solutions often involve a large number of variables, and the interactions between them.

For example, we can train an ML algorithm to recognize human faces by showing it examples. We do not define what a face is, hence the algorithm learns without our direction. The problem is never posed in terms of equations, and in fact the problem may not be expressible in terms of equations. And the algorithm uses an extremely large number of variables to perform this task, including the individual pixels and the interaction between the pixels.

In recent years, ML has become an increasingly useful research tool throughout all fields of scientific research. Examples include drug development, genome research, new materials, and high-energy physics. Consumer products and industrial services have quickly incorporated these technologies, and some of the most valuable companies in the world produce ML-based products and services.

How Is ML Different from Econometric Regressions?

Researchers use traditional regressions to fit a predefined functional form to a set of variables. Regressions are extremely useful when we have a high degree of conviction regarding that functional form and all the interaction effects that bind the variables together. Going back to the eighteenth century, mathematicians developed tools that fit those functional forms using estimators with desirable properties, subject to certain assumptions on the data.

Starting in the 1950s, researchers realized that there was a different way to conduct empirical analyses, with the help of computers. Rather than imposing a functional form, particularly when that form is unknown ex ante, they would allow algorithms to figure out variable dependencies from the data. And rather than making strong assumptions on the data, the algorithms would conduct experiments that evaluate the mathematical properties of out-of-sample predictions. This relaxation in terms of functional form and data assumptions, combined with the use of powerful computers, opened the door to analyzing complex data sets, including highly nonlinear, hierarchical, and noncontinuous interaction effects.

Consider the following example: a researcher wishes to estimate the survival probability of a passenger on the *Titanic*, based on a number of variables, such as gender, ticket class, and age. A typical regression approach would be to fit a logit model to a binary variable, where 1 means survivor and 0 means deceased, using gender, ticket class, and age as regressors. It turns out that, even though these regressors are correct, a logit (or probit) model fails to make good predictions. The reason is that logit models do not recognize that this data set embeds a hierarchical (treelike) structure, with complex interactions. For example, adult males in second class died at a much higher rate than each of these attributes taken independently. In contrast, a simple "classification tree" algorithm performs substantially better, because we allow the algorithm to find that hierarchical structure (and associated complex interactions) for us.

As it turns out, hierarchical structures are omnipresent in economics and finance (Simon 1962). Think of sector classifications, credit ratings, asset classes, economic linkages, trade networks, clusters of regional economies, etc. When confronted with these kinds of problems, ML tools can complement and overcome the limitations of econometrics or similar traditional statistical methods.

How Is ML Different from Big Data?

The term *big data* refers to data sets that are so large and/or complex that traditional statistical techniques fail to extract and model the information contained in them. It is estimated that 90% of all recorded data have been created over the past two years, and 80% of the data is unstructured (i.e., not directly amenable to traditional statistical techniques).

In recent years, the quantity and granularity of economic data have improved dramatically. The good news is that the sudden explosion of administrative, private sector, and micro-level data sets offers an unparalleled insight into the inner workings of the economy. The bad news is that these data sets pose multiple challenges to the study of economics. (1) Some of the most interesting data sets are unstructured. They can also be nonnumerical and noncategorical, like news articles, voice recordings, or satellite images. (2) These data sets are high-dimensional (e.g., credit card transactions.) The number of variables involved often greatly exceeds the number of observations, making it very difficult to apply linear algebra solutions. (3) Many of these data sets are extremely sparse. For instance, samples may contain a large proportion of zeros, where standard notions such as correlation do not work well. (4) Embedded within these data sets is critical information regarding networks of agents, incentives, and aggregate behavior of groups of people. ML techniques are designed for analyzing big data, which is why they are often cited together.

Perhaps the most popular application of ML in asset management is price prediction. But there are plenty of equally important applications, like hedging, portfolio construction, detection of outliers and structural breaks, credit ratings, sentiment analysis, market making, bet sizing, securities taxonomy, and many others. These are real-life applications that transcend the hype often associated with expectations of price prediction.

For example, factor investing firms use ML to redefine value. A few years ago, price-to-earnings ratios may have provided a good ranking for value, but that is not the case nowadays. Today, the notion of value is much more nuanced. Modern asset managers use ML to identify the traits of value, and how those traits interact with momentum, quality, size, etc. Meta-labeling (Section 5.5) is another hot topic that can help asset managers size and time their factor bets.

High-frequency trading firms have utilized ML for years to analyze real-time exchange feeds, in search for footprints left by informed traders. They can utilize this information to make short-term price predictions or to make decisions on the aggressiveness or passiveness in order execution. Credit rating agencies are also strong adopters of ML, as these algorithms have demonstrated their ability to replicate the ratings generated by credit analysts. Outlier detection is another important application, since financial models can be very sensitive to the presence of even a small number of outliers. ML models can help improve investment performance by finding the proper size of a position, leaving the buy-or-sell decision to traditional or fundamental models.

And Quantitative Investors Specifically?

All of the above applications, and many more, are relevant to quantitative investors. It is a great time to be a quant. Data are more abundant than ever, and computers are finally delivering the power needed to make effective use of ML. I am particularly excited about real-time prediction of macroeconomic statistics, following the example of MIT's Billion Prices Project (Cavallo and Rigobon 2016). ML can be specially helpful at uncovering relationships that until now remained hidden, even in traditional data sets. For instance, the economic relationships between companies may not be effectively described by traditional sector-group-industry classifications, such as GICS.[6] A network approach, where companies are related according to a variety of factors, is likely

---

[6] www.msci.com/gics.

to offer a richer and more accurate representation of the dynamics, strengths, and vulnerabilities of specific segments of the stock or credit markets (Cohen and Frazzini 2008).

What Are Some of the Ways That ML Can Be Applied to Investor Portfolios?

Portfolio construction is an extremely promising area for ML (Section 7). For many decades, the asset management industry has relied on variations and refinements of Markowitz's efficient frontier to build investment portfolios. It is known that many of these solutions are optimal in-sample, however, they can perform poorly out-of-sample due to the computational instabilities involved in convex optimization. Numerous classical approaches have attempted, with mixed success, to address these computational instabilities. ML algorithms have shown the potential to produce robust portfolios that perform well out-of-sample, thanks to their ability to recognize sparse hierarchical relationships that traditional methods miss (López de Prado 2016).

What Are the Risks? Is There Anything That Investors Should Be Aware of or Look Out For?

Finance is not a plug-and-play subject as it relates to ML. Modeling financial series is harder than driving cars or recognizing faces. The reason is, the signal-to-noise ratio in financial data is extremely low, as a result of arbitrage forces and nonstationary systems. The computational power and functional flexibility of ML ensures that it will always find a pattern in the data, even if that pattern is a fluke rather than the result of a persistent phenomenon. An "oracle" approach to financial ML, where algorithms are developed to form predictions divorced from all economic theory, is likely to yield false discoveries. I have never heard a scientist say "Forget about theory, I have this oracle that can answer anything, so let's all stop thinking, and let's just believe blindly whatever comes out."

It is important for investors to recognize that ML is not a substitute for economic theory, but rather a powerful tool for building modern economic theories. We need ML to develop better financial theories, and we need financial theories to restrict ML's propensity to overfit. Without this theory–ML interplay, investors are placing their trust on high-tech horoscopes.

How Do You Expect ML to Impact the Asset Management Industry in the Next Decade?

Today, the amount of ML used by farmers is staggering: self-driving tractors, drones scanning for irregular patches of land, sensors feeding cattle and administering nutrients as needed, genetically engineered crops, satellite images for estimating yields, etc. Similarly, I think in ten years we will look back, and ML will be an important aspect of asset management. And just like in the farming industry, although this transformation may not happen overnight, it is clear that there is only one direction forward.

Economic data sets will only get bigger, and computers will only get more powerful. Most asset managers will fail either by not evolving or by rushing into the unknown without fully recognizing the dangers involved in the "oracle" approach. Only a few asset managers will succeed by evolving in a thoughtful and responsible manner.

How Do You Expect ML to Impact Financial Academia in the Next Decade?

Imagine if physicists had to produce theories in a universe where the fundamental laws of nature are in a constant flux; where publications have an impact on the very phenomenon under study; where experimentation is virtually impossible; where data are costly, the signal is dim, and the system under study is incredibly complex ... I feel utmost admiration for how much financial academics have achieved in the face of paramount adversity.

ML has a lot to offer to the academic profession. First, ML provides the power and flexibility needed to find dim signals in the sea of noise caused by arbitrage forces. Second, ML allows academics to decouple the research process into two stages: (1) search for important variables irrespective of functional form, and (2) search for a functional form that binds those variables. López de Prado (2019b) demonstrates how even small specification errors mislead researchers into rejecting important variables. It is hard to overstate the relevance of decoupling the specification search from the variables search. Third, ML offers the possibility of conducting simulations on synthetic data. This is as close as finance will ever get to experimentation, in the absence of laboratories. We live an exciting time to do academic research on financial systems, and I expect tremendous breakthroughs as more financial researchers embrace ML.

Isn't Financial ML All about Price Prediction?

One of the greatest misunderstandings I perceive from reading the press is the notion that ML's main (if not only) objective is price prediction. Asset pricing is undoubtedly a very worthy endeavor, however its importance is often overstated. Having an edge at price prediction is just one necessary, however entirely insufficient, condition to be successful in today's highly competitive market. Other areas that are equally important are data processing, portfolio construction, risk management, monitoring for structural breaks, bet sizing, and detection of false investment strategies, just to cite a few.

Consider the players at the World Series of Poker. The cards are shuffled and distributed randomly. These players obviously cannot predict what cards will be handed to players with any meaningful accuracy. And yet, the same handful of players ends up in top positions year after year. One reason is, bet sizing is more important than card prediction. When a player receives a good hand, he evaluates the probability that another player may hold a strong hand too, and bets strategically. Likewise, investors may not be able to predict prices, however they may recognize when an out-of-the-normal price has printed, and bet accordingly. I am not saying that bet sizing is the key to successful investing. I am merely stating that bet sizing is at least as important as price prediction, and that portfolio construction is arguably even more important.

Why Don't You Discuss a Wide Range of ML Algorithms?

The purpose of this Element is not to introduce the reader to the vast population of ML algorithms used today in finance. There are two reasons for that. First, there are lengthy textbooks dedicated to the systematic exposition of those algorithms, and another one is hardly needed. Excellent references include James et al. (2013), Hastie et al. (2016), and Efron and Hastie (2016). Second, financial data sets have specific nuisances, and the success or failure of a project rests on understanding them. Once we have engineered the features and posed the problem correctly, choosing an algorithm plays a relatively secondary role.

Allow me to illustrate the second point with an example. Compare an algorithm that forecasted a change of 1, but received a realized change of 3, with another algorithm that forecasted a change of -1, but received a realized change of 1. In both cases, the forecast error is 2. In many industrial applications, we would be indifferent between both errors. That is not the case in finance. In the first instance, an investor makes one-third of the predicted profit, whereas in the second instance the investor suffers a loss equal to the predicted profit. Failing to predict the size is an opportunity loss, but failing to predict the sign is an actual loss. Investors penalize actual losses much more than opportunity losses. Predicting the sign of an outcome is often more important than predicting its size, and a reason for favoring classifiers over regression methods in finance. In addition, it is common in finance to find that the sign and size of an outcome depend on different features, so jointly forecasting the sign and size of an outcome with a unique set of features can lead to subpar results.[7] ML experts who transition into finance from other fields often make fundamental mistakes, like posing problems incorrectly, as explained in López de Prado (2018b). Financial ML is a subject in its own right, and the discussion of generic ML algorithms is not the heart of the matter.

Why Don't You Discuss a Specific Investment Strategy,
Like Many Other Books Do?

There are plenty of books in the market that provide recipes for implementing someone else's investment strategy. Those cookbooks show us how to prepare someone else's cake. This Element is different. I want to show you how you can use ML to discover new economic and financial theories that are relevant to you, on which you can base your proprietary investment strategies. Your investment strategies are just the particular implementation of the theories that first you must discover independently. You cannot bake someone else's cake and expect to retain it for yourself.

1.10 Conclusions

The purpose of this Element is to introduce ML tools that are useful for discovering economic and financial theories. Successful investment strategies are specific implementations of general theories. An investment strategy that lacks a theoretical justification is likely to be false. Hence, a researcher should concentrate her efforts on developing a theory, rather than of backtesting potential strategies.

ML is not a black box, and it does not necessarily overfit. ML tools complement rather than replace the classical statistical methods. Some of ML's strengths include (1) Focus on out-of-sample predictability over variance adjudication; (2) usage of computational methods to avoid relying on (potentially unrealistic) assumptions; (3) ability to "learn" complex specifications, including nonlinear, hierarchical, and noncontinuous interaction effects in a high-dimensional space; and (4) ability to disentangle the variable search from the specification search, in a manner robust to multicollinearity and other substitution effects.

---

[7] See López de Prado (2018a) for a discussion of meta-labeling algorithms, where the sign and size decision is made by independent algorithms.

1.11 Exercises

1 Can quantitative methods be used to predict events that never happened before? How could quantitative methods predict a black swan?

2 Why is theory particularly important in finance and economics? What is the best use of ML in finance?

3 What are popular misconceptions about financial ML? Are financial data sets large enough for ML applications?

4 How does ML control for overfitting? Is the signal-to-noise ratio too low in finance for allowing the use of ML?

5 Describe a quantitative approach in finance that combines classical and ML methods. How is ML different from a large regression? Describe five applications of financial ML.

2 Denoising and Detoning

2.1 Motivation

Covariance matrices are ubiquitous in finance. We use them to run regressions, estimate risks, optimize portfolios, simulate scenarios via Monte Carlo, find clusters, reduce the dimensionality of a vector space, and so on. Empirical covariance matrices are computed on series of observations from a random vector, in order to estimate the linear comovement between the random variables that constitute the random vector. Given the finite and nondeterministic nature of these observations, the estimate of the covariance matrix includes some amount of noise. Empirical covariance matrices derived from estimated factors are also numerically ill-conditioned, because those factors are also estimated from flawed data. Unless we treat this noise, it will impact the calculations we perform with the covariance matrix, sometimes to the point of rendering the analysis useless.

The goal of this section is to explain a procedure for reducing the noise and enhancing the signal included in an empirical covariance matrix. Throughout this Element, we assume that empirical covariance and correlation matrices have been subjected to this procedure.

2.2 The Marcenko–Pastur Theorem

Consider a matrix of independent and identically distributed random observations X, of size TxN, where the underlying process generating the observations has zero mean and variance σ^2. The matrix $C = T^{-1}X'X$ has eigenvalues λ that asymptotically converge (as $N \to +\infty$ and $T \to +\infty$ with $1 < {}^T/_N < +\infty$) to the Marcenko–Pastur probability density function (PDF),

$$f[\lambda] = \begin{cases} \dfrac{T}{N} \dfrac{\sqrt{(\lambda_+ - \lambda)(\lambda - \lambda_-)}}{2\pi\lambda\sigma^2} & \text{if } \lambda \in [\lambda_-, \lambda_+] \\ 0 & \text{if } \lambda \notin [\lambda_-, \lambda_+], \end{cases}$$

where the maximum expected eigenvalue is $\lambda_+ = \sigma^2 \left(1 + \sqrt{N/T}\right)^2$ and the minimum expected eigenvalue is $\lambda_- = \sigma^2 \left(1 - \sqrt{N/T}\right)^2$. When $\sigma^2 = 1$, then C is the correlation matrix associated with X. Code Snippet 2.1 implements the Marcenko–Pastur PDF in python.

Eigenvalues $\lambda \in [\lambda_-, \lambda_+]$ are consistent with random behavior, and eigenvalues $\lambda \notin [\lambda_-, \lambda_+]$ are consistent with nonrandom behavior. Specifically, we associate eigenvalues $\lambda \in [0, \lambda_+]$ with noise. Figure 2.1 and Code Snippet 2.2 demonstrate how closely the Marcenko–Pastur distribution explains the eigenvalues of a random matrix X.

SNIPPET 2.1 THE MARCENKO–PASTUR PDF

```
import numpy as np,pandas as pd
#-------------------------------------------------------
def mpPDF(var,q,pts):
  # Marcenko-Pastur pdf
  # q=T/N
  eMin,eMax=var*(1-(1./q)**.5)**2,var*(1+(1./q)**.5)**2
  eVal=np.linspace(eMin,eMax,pts)
  pdf=q/(2*np.pi*var*eVal)*((eMax-eVal)*(eVal-eMin))**.5
  pdf=pd.Series(pdf,index=eVal)
  return pdf
```

SNIPPET 2.2 TESTING THE MARCENKO–PASTUR THEOREM

```
from sklearn.neighbors.kde import KernelDensity
#-------------------------------------------------------
def getPCA(matrix):
  # Get eVal,eVec from a Hermitian matrix
  eVal,eVec=np.linalg.eigh(matrix)
  indices=eVal.argsort()[::-1] # arguments for sorting eVal desc
  eVal,eVec=eVal[indices],eVec[:,indices]
  eVal=np.diagflat(eVal)
  return eVal,eVec
#-------------------------------------------------------
def fitKDE(obs,bWidth=.25,kernel='gaussian',x=None):
  # Fit kernel to a series of obs, and derive the prob of obs
  # x is the array of values on which the fit KDE will be evaluated
  if len(obs.shape)==1:obs=obs.reshape(-1,1)
  kde=KernelDensity(kernel=kernel,bandwidth=bWidth).fit(obs)
  if x is None:x=np.unique(obs).reshape(-1,1)
  if len(x.shape)==1:x=x.reshape(-1,1)
  logProb=kde.score_samples(x) # log(density)
  pdf=pd.Series(np.exp(logProb),index=x.flatten())
  return pdf
#-------------------------------------------------------
x=np.random.normal(size=(10000,1000))
eVal0,eVec0=getPCA(np.corrcoef(x,rowvar=0))
pdf0=mpPDF(1.,q=x.shape[0]/float(x.shape[1]),pts=1000)
pdf1=fitKDE(np.diag(eVal0),bWidth=.01) # empirical pdf
```

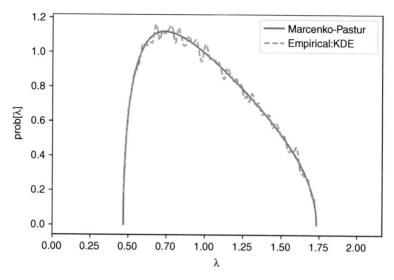

Figure 2.1 A visualization of the Marcenko–Pastur theorem.

2.3 Random Matrix with Signal

In an empirical correlation matrix, not all eigenvectors may be random. Code Snippet 2.3 builds a covariance matrix that is not perfectly random, and hence its eigenvalues will only approximately follow the Marcenko–Pastur PDF. Out of the nCols random variables that form the covariance matrix generated by getRndCov, only nFact contain some signal. To further dilute the signal, we add that covariance matrix to a purely random matrix, with a weight alpha. See Lewandowski et al. (2009) for alternative ways of building a random covariance matrix.

2.4 Fitting the Marcenko–Pastur Distribution

In this section, we follow the approach introduced by Laloux et al. (2000). Since only part of the variance is caused by random eigenvectors, we can adjust σ^2 accordingly in the above equations. For instance, if we assume that the eigenvector associated with the highest eigenvalue is *not* random, then we should replace σ^2 with $\sigma^2(1 - \lambda_+/N)$ in the above equations. In fact, we can fit the function $f[\lambda]$ to the empirical distribution of the eigenvalues to derive the implied σ^2. That will give us the variance that is explained by the random eigenvectors present in the correlation matrix, and it will determine the cutoff level λ_+, adjusted for the presence of nonrandom eigenvectors.

Code Snippet 2.4 fits the Marcenko–Pastur PDF to a random covariance matrix that contains signal. The objective of the fit is to find the value of σ^2 that minimizes the sum of the squared differences between the analytical PDF and

Snippet 2.3 Add Signal to a Random Covariance Matrix

```
def getRndCov(nCols,nFacts):
  w=np.random.normal(size=(nCols,nFacts))
  cov=np.dot(w,w.T) # random cov matrix, however not full rank
  cov+=np.diag(np.random.uniform(size=nCols)) # full rank cov
  return cov
#-------------------------------------------------------------
def cov2corr(cov):
  # Derive the correlation matrix from a covariance matrix
  std=np.sqrt(np.diag(cov))
  corr=cov/np.outer(std,std)
  corr[corr<-1],corr[corr>1]=-1,1 # numerical error
  return corr
#-------------------------------------------------------------
alpha,nCols,nFact,q=.995,1000,100,10
cov=np.cov(np.random.normal(size=(nCols*q,nCols)),rowvar=0)
cov=alpha*cov+(1-alpha)*getRndCov(nCols,nFact) # noise+signal
corr0=cov2corr(cov)
eVal0,eVec0=getPCA(corr0)
```

Snippet 2.4 Fitting the Marcenko–Pastur PDF

```
from scipy.optimize import minimize
#-------------------------------------------------------------
def errPDFs(var,eVal,q,bWidth,pts=1000):
  # Fit error
  pdf0=mpPDF(var,q,pts) # theoretical pdf
  pdf1=fitKDE(eVal,bWidth,x=pdf0.index.values) # empirical pdf
  sse=np.sum((pdf1-pdf0)**2)
  return sse
#-------------------------------------------------------------
def findMaxEval(eVal,q,bWidth):
  # Find max random eVal by fitting Marcenko's dist
  out=minimize(lambda *x:errPDFs(*x),.5,args=(eVal,q,bWidth),
    bounds=((1E-5,1-1E-5),))
  if out['success']:var=out['x'][0]
  else:var=1
  eMax=var*(1+(1./q)**.5)**2
  return eMax,var
#-------------------------------------------------------------
eMax0,var0=findMaxEval(np.diag(eVal0),q,bWidth=.01)
nFacts0=eVal0.shape[0]-np.diag(eVal0)[::-1].searchsorted(eMax0)
```

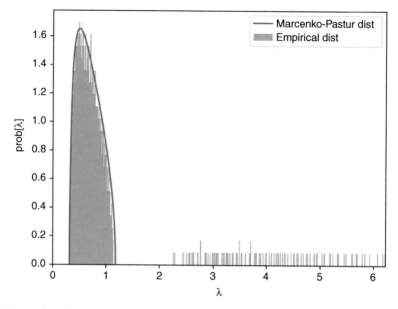

Figure 2.2 Fitting the Marcenko–Pastur PDF on a noisy covariance matrix.

the kernel density estimate (KDE) of the observed eigenvalues (for references on KDE, see Rosenblatt 1956; Parzen 1962). The value λ_+ is reported as eMax0, the value of σ^2 is stored as var0, and the number of factors is recovered as nFacts0.

Figure 2.2 plots the histogram of eigenvalues and the PDF of the fitted Marcenko–Pastur distribution. Eigenvalues to the right of the fitted Marcenko–Pastur distribution cannot be associated with noise, thus they are related to signal. The code returns a value of 100 for nFacts0, the same number of factors we had injected to the covariance matrix. Despite the dim signal present in the covariance matrix, the procedure has been able to separate the eigenvalues associated with noise from the eigenvalues associated with signal. The fitted distribution implies that $\sigma^2 \approx .6768$, indicating that only about 32.32% of the variance can be attributed to signal. This is one way of measuring the signal-to-noise ratio in financial data sets, which is known to be low as a result of arbitrage forces.

2.5 Denoising

It is common in financial applications to shrink a numerically ill-conditioned covariance matrix (Ledoit and Wolf 2004). By making the covariance matrix closer to a diagonal, shrinkage reduces its condition number. However, shrinkage accomplishes that without discriminating between noise and signal. As a result, shrinkage can further eliminate an already weak signal.

In the previous section, we have learned how to discriminate between eigenvalues associated with noise components and eigenvalues associated with signal components. In this section we discuss how to use this information for denoising the correlation matrix.

2.5.1 Constant Residual Eigenvalue Method

This approach consists in setting a constant eigenvalue for all random eigenvectors. Let $\{\lambda_n\}_{n=1,\dots,N}$ be the set of all eigenvalues, ordered descending, and i be the position of the eigenvalue such that $\lambda_i > \lambda_+$ and $\lambda_{i+1} \leq \lambda_+$. Then we set $\lambda_j = 1/(N-i) \sum_{k=i+1}^{N} \lambda_k, j = i+1, \dots, N$, hence preserving the trace of the correlation matrix. Given the eigenvector decomposition $VW = W\Lambda$, we form the denoised correlation matrix C_1 as

$$\widetilde{C}_1 = W\widetilde{\Lambda}W'$$

$$C_1 = \widetilde{C}_1 \left[\left(\text{diag}\left[\widetilde{C}_1\right] \right)^{\frac{1}{2}} \left(\text{diag}\left[\widetilde{C}_1\right] \right)^{\frac{1}{2}'} \right]^{-1},$$

where $\widetilde{\Lambda}$ is the diagonal matrix holding the corrected eigenvalues, the apostrophe (') transposes a matrix, and diag[.] zeroes all non-diagonal elements of a squared matrix. The reason for the second transformation is to rescale the matrix $\widetilde{C}_1$, so that the main diagonal of C_1 is an array of 1s. Code Snippet 2.5 implements this method. Figure 2.3 compares the logarithms of the eigenvalues before and after denoising by this method.

SNIPPET 2.5 DENOISING BY CONSTANT RESIDUAL EIGENVALUE

```
def denoisedCorr(eVal,eVec,nFacts):
 # Remove noise from corr by fixing random eigenvalues
 eVal_=np.diag(eVal).copy()
 eVal_[nFacts:]=eVal_[nFacts:].sum()/float(eVal_.shape[0]-nFacts)
 eVal_=np.diag(eVal_)
 corr1=np.dot(eVec,eVal_).dot(eVec.T)
 corr1=cov2corr(corr1)
 return corr1
#- - - - - - - - - - - - - - - - - - - - - - - - - - - - - - - - - - - -
corr1=denoisedCorr(eVal0,eVec0,nFacts0)
eVal1,eVec1=getPCA(corr1)
```

2.5.2 Targeted Shrinkage

The numerical method described earlier is preferable to shrinkage, because it removes the noise while preserving the signal. Alternatively, we could target the

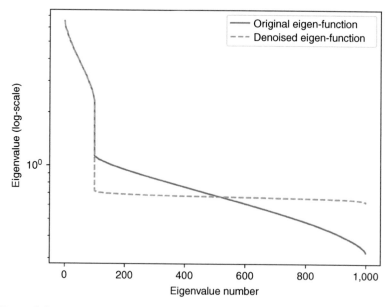

Figure 2.3 A comparison of eigenvalues before and after applying the residual eigenvalue method.

application of the shrinkage strictly to the random eigenvectors. Consider the correlation matrix C_1

$$C_1 = W_L \Lambda_L W_L' + \alpha W_R \Lambda_R W_R' + (1 - \alpha) \text{diag}[W_R \Lambda_R W_R'],$$

where W_R and Λ_R are the eigenvectors and eigenvalues associated with $\{n | \lambda_n \leq \lambda_+\}$, W_L and Λ_L are the eigenvectors and eigenvalues associated with $\{n | \lambda_n > \lambda_+\}$, and α regulates the amount of shrinkage among the eigenvectors and eigenvalues associated with noise ($\alpha \to 0$ for total shrinkage). Code Snippet 2.6 implements this method. Figure 2.4 compares the logarithms of the eigenvalues before and after denoising by this method.

2.6 Detoning

Financial correlation matrices usually incorporate a market component. The market component is characterized by the first eigenvector, with loadings $W_{n,1} \approx N^{-\frac{1}{2}}$, $n = 1, \ldots, N$. Accordingly, a market component affects every item of the covariance matrix. In the context of clustering applications, it is useful to remove the market component, if it exists (a hypothesis that can be tested statistically). The reason is, it is more difficult to cluster a correlation

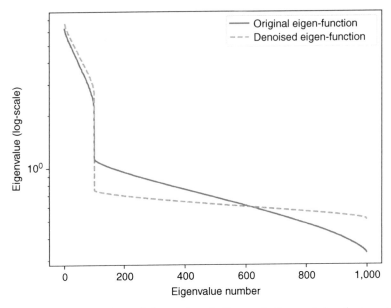

Figure 2.4 A comparison of eigenvalues before and after applying the targeted shrinkage method.

SNIPPET 2.6 DENOISING BY TARGETED SHRINKAGE

```
def denoisedCorr2(eVal,eVec,nFacts,alpha=0):
  # Remove noise from corr through targeted shrinkage
  eValL,eVecL=eVal[:nFacts,:nFacts],eVec[:,:nFacts]
  eValR,eVecR=eVal[nFacts:,nFacts:],eVec[:,nFacts:]
  corr0=np.dot(eVecL,eValL).dot(eVecL.T)
  corr1=np.dot(eVecR,eValR).dot(eVecR.T)
  corr2=corr0+alpha*corr1+(1-alpha)*np.diag(np.diag(corr1))
  return corr2
#- - - - - - - - - - - - - - - - - - - - - - - - - - - - - - - - - - - - - - -
corr1=denoisedCorr2(eVal0,eVec0,nFacts0,alpha=.5)
eVal1,eVec1=getPCA(corr1)
```

matrix with a strong market component, because the algorithm will struggle to find dissimilarities *across* clusters. By removing the market component, we allow a greater portion of the correlation to be explained by components that affect specific subsets of the securities. It is similar to removing a loud tone that prevents us from hearing other sounds. Detoning is the principal components analysis analogue to computing beta-adjusted (or market-adjusted) returns in regression analysis.

We can remove the market component from the denoised correlation matrix, C_1, to form the detoned correlation matrix

$$\tilde{C}_2 = C_1 - W_M \Lambda_M W_M' = W_D \Lambda_D W_D'$$

$$C_2 = \tilde{C}_2 \left[\left(\mathrm{diag} \left[\tilde{C}_2 \right] \right)^{1/2} \left(\mathrm{diag} \left[\tilde{C}_2 \right] \right)^{1/2'} \right]^{-1},$$

where W_M and Λ_M are the eigenvectors and eigenvalues associated with market components (usually only one, but possibly more), and W_D and Λ_D are the eigenvectors and eigenvalues associated with nonmarket components.

The detoned correlation matrix is singular, as a result of eliminating (at least) one eigenvector. This is not a problem for clustering applications, as most approaches do not require the invertibility of the correlation matrix. Still, a detoned correlation matrix C_2 cannot be used directly for mean-variance portfolio optimization. Instead, we can optimize a portfolio on the selected (nonzero) principal components, and map the optimal allocations f^* back to the original basis. The optimal allocations in the original basis are

$$\omega^* = W_+ f^*,$$

where W_+ contains only the eigenvectors that survived the detoning process (i.e., with a nonnull eigenvalue), and f^* is the vector of optimal allocations to those same components.

2.7 Experimental Results

Working with denoised and detoned covariance matrices renders substantial benefits. Those benefits result from the mathematical properties of those treated matrices, and can be evaluated through Monte Carlo experiments. In this section we discuss two characteristic portfolios of the efficient frontier, namely, the minimum variance and maximum Sharpe ratio solutions, since any member of the unconstrained efficient frontier can be derived as a convex combination of the two.

2.7.1 Minimum Variance Portfolio

In this section, we compute the errors associated with estimating a minimum variance portfolio with and without denoising. Code Snippet 2.7 forms a vector of means and a covariance matrix out of ten blocks of size fifty each, where off-diagonal elements within each block have a correlation of 0.5. This covariance matrix is a stylized representation of a true (nonempirical) detoned correlation matrix of the S&P 500, where each block is associated with an economic sector. Without loss of generality, the variances are drawn from a uniform distribution

SNIPPET 2.7 GENERATING A BLOCK-DIAGONAL COVARIANCE MATRIX AND A VECTOR OF MEANS

```
def formBlockMatrix(nBlocks,bSize,bCorr):
  block=np.ones((bSize,bSize))*bCorr
  block[range(bSize),range(bSize)]=1
  corr=block_diag(*([block]*nBlocks))
  return corr
#-------------------------------------------------------
def formTrueMatrix(nBlocks,bSize,bCorr):
  corr0=formBlockMatrix(nBlocks,bSize,bCorr)
  corr0=pd.DataFrame(corr0)
  cols=corr0.columns.tolist()
  np.random.shuffle(cols)
  corr0=corr0[cols].loc[cols].copy(deep=True)
  std0=np.random.uniform(.05,.2,corr0.shape[0])
  cov0=corr2cov(corr0,std0)
  mu0=np.random.normal(std0,std0,cov0.shape[0]).reshape(-1,1)
  return mu0,cov0
#-------------------------------------------------------
from scipy.linalg import block_diag
from sklearn.covariance import LedoitWolf
nBlocks,bSize,bCorr=10,50,.5
np.random.seed(0)
mu0,cov0=formTrueMatrix(nBlocks,bSize,bCorr)
```

bounded between 5% and 20%, and the vector of means is drawn from a Normal distribution with mean and standard deviation equal to the standard deviation from the covariance matrix. This is consistent with the notion that in an efficient market all securities have the same expected Sharpe ratio. We fix a seed to facilitate the comparison of results across runs with different parameters.

Code Snippet 2.8 uses the true (nonempirical) covariance matrix to draw a random matrix X of size TxN, and it derives the associated empirical covariance matrix and vector of means. Function simCovMu receives argument nObs,

SNIPPET 2.8 GENERATING THE EMPIRICAL COVARIANCE MATRIX

```
def simCovMu(mu0,cov0,nObs,shrink=False):
  x=np.random.multivariate_normal(mu0.flatten(),cov0,size=nObs)
  mu1=x.mean(axis=0).reshape(-1,1)
  if shrink:cov1=LedoitWolf().fit(x).covariance_
  else:cov1=np.cov(x,rowvar=0)
  return mu1,cov1
```

which sets the value of T. When shrink=True, the function performs a Ledoit–Wolf shrinkage of the empirical covariance matrix.

Code Snippet 2.9 applies the methods explained in this section, to denoise the empirical covariance matrix. In this particular experiment, we denoise through the constant residual eigenvalue method.

SNIPPET 2.9 DENOISING OF THE EMPIRICAL COVARIANCE MATRIX

```
def corr2cov(corr,std):
  cov=corr*np.outer(std,std)
  return cov
#- - - - - - - - - - - - - - - - - - - - - - - - - - - - - - - - - - - - - - - -
def deNoiseCov(cov0,q,bWidth):
  corr0=cov2corr(cov0)
  eVal0,eVec0=getPCA(corr0)
  eMax0,var0=findMaxEval(np.diag(eVal0),q,bWidth)
  nFacts0=eVal0.shape[0]-np.diag(eVal0)[::-1].searchsorted(eMax0)
  corr1=denoisedCorr(eVal0,eVec0,nFacts0)
  cov1=corr2cov(corr1,np.diag(cov0)**.5)
  return cov1
```

Code Snippet 2.10 runs the following Monte Carlo experiment with 1,000 iterations: (1) draw a random empirical covariance matrix (shrinkage optional) with $T = 1,000$; (2) denoise the empirical covariance matrix (optional); (3)

SNIPPET 2.10 DENOISING OF THE EMPIRICAL COVARIANCE MATRIX

```
def optPort(cov,mu=None):
  inv=np.linalg.inv(cov)
  ones=np.ones(shape=(inv.shape[0],1))
  if mu is None:mu=ones
  w=np.dot(inv,mu)
  w/=np.dot(ones.T,w)
  return w
#- - - - - - - - - - - - - - - - - - - - - - - - - - - - - - - - - - - - - - -
nObs,nTrials,bWidth,shrink,minVarPortf=1000,1000,.01,False,True
w1=pd.DataFrame(columns=xrange(cov0.shape[0]),
                index=xrange(nTrials),dtype=float)
w1_d=w1.copy(deep=True)
np.random.seed(0)
for i in range(nTrials):
  mu1,cov1=simCovMu(mu0,cov0,nObs,shrink=shrink)
  if minVarPortf:mu1=None
  cov1_d=deNoiseCov(cov1,nObs*1./cov1.shape[1],bWidth)
  w1.loc[i]=optPort(cov1,mu1).flatten()
  w1_d.loc[i]=optPort(cov1_d,mu1).flatten()
```

derive the minimum variance portfolio, using the function optPort. When we pass the argument shrink=True to function simCovMu, the covariance matrix is shrunk. When parameter bWidth>0, the covariance matrix is denoised prior to estimating the minimum variance portfolio.[8] A random seed is arbitrarily set, so that we may run this Monte Carlo experiment on the same covariance matrices, with and without denoising.

Code Snippet 2.11 computes the true minimum variance portfolio, derived from the true covariance matrix. Using those allocations as benchmark, it then computes the root-mean-square errors (RMSE) across all weights, with and without denoising. We can run Code Snippet 2.11 with and without shrinkage, thus obtaining the four combinations displayed in Figure 2.5. Denoising is much more effective than shrinkage: the denoised minimum variance portfolio incurs only 40.15% of the RMSE incurred by the minimum variance portfolio without denoising. That is a 59.85% reduction in RMSE from denoising alone, compared to a 30.22% reduction using Ledoit–Wolf shrinkage. Shrinkage adds little benefit beyond what denoising contributes. The reduction in RMSE from combining denoising with shrinkage is 65.63%, which is not much better than the result from using denoising only.

SNIPPET 2.11 ROOT-MEAN-SQUARE ERRORS

```
w0=optPort(cov0,None if minVarPortf else mu0)
w0=np.repeat(w0.T,w1.shape[0],axis=0)
rmsd=np.mean((w1-w0).values.flatten()**2)**.5 # RMSE
rmsd_d=np.mean((w1_d-w0).values.flatten()**2)**.5 # RMSE
print rmsd,rmsd_d
```

	Not denoised	Denoised
Not shrunk	4.95E–03	1.99E–03
Shrunk	3.45E–03	1.70E–03

Figure 2.5 RMSE for combinations of denoising and shrinkage (minimum variance portfolio).

2.7.2 Maximum Sharpe Ratio Portfolio

We can repeat the previous experiment, where on this occasion we target the estimation of the maximum Sharpe ratio portfolio. In order to do that, we need

---

[8] As an exercise, we leave the estimation via cross-validation of the optimal value of bWidth.

to set minVarPortf=True in Code Snippet 2.10. Figure 2.6 shows that, once again, denoising is much more effective than shrinkage: the denoised maximum Sharpe ratio portfolio incurs only 0.04% of the RMSE incurred by the maximum Sharpe ratio portfolio without denoising. That is a 94.44% reduction in RMSE from denoising alone, compared to a 70.77% reduction using Ledoit–Wolf shrinkage. While shrinkage is somewhat helpful in absence of denoising, it adds no benefit in combination with denoising. This is because shrinkage dilutes the noise at the expense of diluting some of the signal as well.

	Not denoised	Denoised
Not shrunk	9.48E–01	5.27E–02
Shrunk	2.77E–01	5.17E–02

Figure 2.6 RMSE for combinations of denoising and shrinkage (maximum Sharpe ratio portfolio).

2.8 Conclusions

In finance, empirical covariance matrices are often numerically ill-conditioned, as a result of the small number of independent observations used to estimate a large number of parameters. Working with those matrices directly, without treatment, is not recommended. Even if the covariance matrix is nonsingular, and therefore invertible, the small determinant all but guarantees that the estimations error will be greatly magnified by the inversion process. These estimation errors cause misallocation of assets and substantial transaction costs due to unnecessary rebalancing.

The Marcenko–Pastur theorem gives us the distribution of the eigenvalues associated with a random matrix. By fitting this distribution, we can discriminate between eigenvalues associated with signal and eigenvalues associated with noise. The latter can be adjusted to correct the matrix's ill-conditioning, without diluting the signal. This random matrix theoretic approach is generally preferable to (1) the threshold method (Jolliffe 2002, 113), which selects a number of components that jointly explain a fixed amount of variance, regardless of the true amount of variance caused by noise; and (2) the shrinkage method (Ledoit and Wolf 2004), which can remove some of the noise at the cost of diluting much of the signal.

Recall that the correlation matrix's condition number is the ratio between its maximal and minimal (by moduli) eigenvalues. Denoising reduces the condition number by increasing the lowest eigenvalue. We can further reduce the condition number by reducing the highest eigenvalue. This makes mathematical sense, and also intuitive sense. Removing the market components present in the correlation matrix reinforces the more subtle signals hiding under the market "tone." For example, if we are trying to cluster a correlation matrix of stock returns, detoning that matrix will likely help amplify the signals associated with other exposures, such as sector, industry, or size.

We have demonstrated the usefulness of denoising in the context of portfolio optimization, however its applications extend to any use of the covariance matrix. For example, denoising the matrix $X'X$ before inverting it should help reduce the variance of regression estimates, and improve the power of statistical tests of hypothesis. For the same reason, covariance matrices derived from regressed factors (also known as factor-based covariance matrices) also require denoising, and should not be used without numerical treatment.

2.9 Exercises

1 Implement in python the detoning method described in Section 2.6.
2 Using a series of matrix of stock returns:
   a Compute the covariance matrix. What is the condition number of the correlation matrix?
   b Compute one hundred efficient frontiers by drawing one hundred alternative vectors of expected returns from a Normal distribution with mean 10% and standard deviation 10%.
   c Compute the variance of the errors against the mean efficient frontier.
3 Repeat Exercise 2, where this time you denoise the covariance matrix before computing the one hundred efficient frontiers.
   a What is the value of σ^2 implied by the Marcenko–Pastur distribution?
   b How many eigenvalues are associated with random components?
   c Is the variance of the errors significantly higher or lower? Why?
4 Repeat Exercise 2, where this time you apply the Ledoit–Wolf shrinkage method (instead of denoising) on the covariance matrix before computing the one hundred efficient frontiers. Is the variance of the errors significantly higher or lower? Why?
5 Repeat Exercise 3, where this time you also detone the covariance matrix before computing the one hundred efficient frontiers. Is the variance of the errors significantly higher or lower? Why?
6 What happens if you drop the components whose eigenvalues fall below a given threshold? Can you still compute the efficient frontiers? How?
7 Extend function fitKDE in Code Snippet 2.2, so that it estimates through cross-validation the optimal value of bWidth.

3 Distance Metrics

3.1 Motivation

In Section 2, we have studied important numerical properties of the empirical correlation (and by extension, covariance) matrix. Despite all of its virtues, correlation suffers from some critical limitations as a measure of codependence. In this section, we overcome those limitations by reviewing information theory concepts that underlie many modern marvels, such as the internet, mobile phones, file compression, video streaming, or encryption. None of these inventions would have been possible if researchers had not looked beyond correlations to understand codependency.

As it turns out, information theory in general, and the concept of Shannon's entropy in particular, also have useful applications in finance. The key idea behind entropy is to quantify the amount of uncertainty associated with a random variable. Information theory is also essential to ML, because the primary goal of many ML algorithms is to reduce the amount of uncertainty involved in the solution to a problem. In this section, we review concepts that are used throughout ML in a variety of settings, including (1) defining the objective function in decision tree learning; (2) defining the loss function for classification problems; (3) evaluating the distance between two random variables; (4) comparing clusters; and (5) feature selection.

3.2 A Correlation-Based Metric

Correlation is a useful measure of linear codependence. Once a correlation matrix has been denoised and detoned, it can reveal important structural information about a system. For example, we could use correlations to identify clusters of highly interrelated securities. But before we can do that, we need to address a technical problem: correlation is not a metric, because it does not satisfy nonnegativity and triangle inequality conditions. Metrics are important because they induce an intuitive topology on a set. Without that intuitive topology, comparing non-metric measurements of codependence can lead to rather incoherent outcomes. For instance, the difference between correlations (0.9,1.0) is the same as (0.1,0.2), even though the former involves a greater difference in terms of codependence.

Consider two random vectors X, Y of size T, and a correlation estimate $\rho[X, Y]$, with the only requirement that $\sigma[X, Y] = \rho[X, Y]\sigma[X]\sigma[Y]$, where $\sigma[X, Y]$ is the covariance between the two vectors and $\sigma[.]$ is the standard deviation. Pearson's correlation is one of several correlation estimates that satisfy these requirements. Then, the measure $d_\rho[X, Y] = \sqrt{1/2(1 - \rho[X, Y])}$ is a metric.

To prove that statement, first consider that the Euclidean distance between the two vectors is $d[X, Y] = \sqrt{\sum_{t=1}^{T} (X_t - Y_t)^2}$. Second, we z-standardize those vectors as $x = (X - \overline{X})/\sigma[X]$, $y = (Y - \overline{Y})/\sigma[Y]$, where $\overline{X}$ is the mean of X, and $\overline{Y}$ is the mean of Y. Consequently, $\rho[x, y] = \rho[X, Y]$. Third, we derive the Euclidean distance $d[x, y]$ as

$$
\begin{aligned}
d[x, y] &= \sqrt{\sum_{t=1}^{T} (x_t - y_t)^2} \\
&= \sqrt{\sum_{t=1}^{T} x_t^2 + \sum_{t=1}^{T} y_t^2 - 2\sum_{t=1}^{T} x_t y_t} = \sqrt{T + T - 2T\sigma[x, y]} \\
&= \sqrt{2T\left(1 - \underbrace{\rho[x, y]}_{=\rho[X,Y]}\right)} = \sqrt{4T} d_\rho[X, Y].
\end{aligned}
$$

The implication is that $d_\rho[X, Y]$ is a linear multiple of the Euclidean distance between the vectors $\{X, Y\}$ after z-standardization ($d[x, y]$), hence it inherits the true-metric properties of the Euclidean distance.

The metric $d[x, y]$ has the property that it is normalized, $d_\rho[X, Y] \in [0, 1]$, because $\rho[X, Y] \in [-1, 1]$. Another property is that it deems more distant two random variables with negative correlation than two random variables with positive correlation, regardless of their absolute value. This property makes sense in many applications. For example, we may wish to build a long-only portfolio, where holdings in negative-correlated securities can only offset risk, and therefore should be treated as different for diversification purposes. In other instances, like in long-short portfolios, we often prefer to consider highly negatively correlated securities as similar, because the position sign can override the sign of the correlation. For that case, we can define an alternative normalized correlation-based distance metric, $d_{|\rho|}[X, Y] = \sqrt{1 - |\rho[X, Y]|}$.

Similarly, we can prove that $d_{|\rho|}[X, Y]$ descends to a true metric on the $\mathbb{Z}/2\mathbb{Z}$ quotient. In order to do that, we redefine $y = (Y - \overline{Y})/\sigma[Y]\text{sgn}[\rho[X, Y]]$, where $\text{sgn}[.]$ is the sign operator, so that $0 \leq \rho[x, y] = |\rho[X, Y]|$. Then, following the same argument used earlier,

$$d[x,y] = \sqrt{2T\left(1 - \underbrace{\rho[x,y]}_{=|\rho[X,Y]|}\right)} = \sqrt{2T}d_{|\rho|}[X,Y].$$

3.3 Marginal and Joint Entropy

The notion of correlation presents three important caveats. First, it quantifies the *linear* codependency between two random variables. It neglects nonlinear relationships. Second, correlation is highly influenced by outliers. Third, its application beyond the multivariate Normal case is questionable. We may compute the correlation between any two real variables, however that correlation is typically meaningless unless the two variables follow a bivariate Normal distribution. To overcome these caveats, we need to introduce a few information-theoretic concepts.

Let X be a discrete random variable that takes a value x from the set S_X with probability $p[x]$. The entropy of X is defined as

$$H[X] = -\sum_{x \in S_X} p[x]\log[p[x]],$$

Throughout this section, we will follow the convention that $0\log[0] = 0$, since $\lim_{p \to 0^+} p\log[p] = 0$. The value $1/p[x]$ measures how surprising an observation is, because surprising observations are characterized by their low probability. Entropy is the expected value of those surprises, where the $\log[.]$ function prevents that $p[x]$ cancels $1/p[x]$ and endows entropy with desirable mathematical properties. Accordingly, entropy can be interpreted as the amount of uncertainty associated with X. Entropy is zero when all probability is concentrated in a single element of S_X. Entropy reaches a maximum at $\log[\|S_X\|]$ when X is distributed uniformly, $p[x] = 1/\|S_X\|, \forall x \in S_X$.

Let Y be a discrete random variable that takes a value y from the set S_Y with probability $p[y]$. Random variables X and Y do not need to be defined on the same probability space. The joint entropy of X and Y is

$$H[X,Y] = -\sum_{x,y \in S_X \times S_Y} p[x,y]\log[p[x,y]].$$

In particular, we have that $H[X,Y] = H[Y,X]$, $H[X,X] = H[X]$, $H[X,Y] \geq \max\{H[X], H[Y]\}$, and $H[X,Y] \leq H[X] + H[Y]$.

It is important to recognize that Shannon's entropy is finite only for discrete random variables. In the continuous case, one should use the limiting density of discrete points (LDDP), or discretize the random variable, as explained in Section 3.9 (Jaynes 2003).

3.4 Conditional Entropy

The conditional entropy of X given Y is defined as

$$H[X|Y] = H[X, Y] - H[Y] = - \sum_{y \in S_Y} p[y] \sum_{x \in S_X} p[x|Y = y] \log[p[x|Y = y]],$$

where $p[x|Y = y]$ is the probability that X takes the value x conditioned on Y having taken the value y. Following this definition, $H[X|Y]$ is the uncertainty we expect in X if we are told the value of Y. Accordingly, $H[X|X] = 0$, and $H[X] \geq H[X|Y]$.

3.5 Kullback–Leibler Divergence

Let p and q be two discrete probability distributions defined on the same probability space. The Kullback–Leibler (or KL) divergence between p and q is

$$D_{KL}[p \| q] = - \sum_{x \in S_X} p[x] \log \left[\frac{q[x]}{p[x]} \right] = \sum_{x \in S_X} p[x] \log \left[\frac{p[x]}{q[x]} \right],$$

where $q[x] = 0 \Rightarrow p[x] = 0$. Intuitively, this expression measures how much p diverges from a reference distribution q. The KL divergence is *not* a metric: although it is always nonnegative $(D_{KL}[p \| q] \geq 0)$, it violates the symmetry $(D_{KL}[p \| q] \neq D_{KL}[q \| p])$ and triangle inequality conditions. Note the difference with the definition of joint entropy, where the two random variables did not necessarily exist in the same probability space. KL divergence is widely used in variational inference.

3.6 Cross-Entropy

Let p and q be two discrete probability distributions defined on the same probability space. Cross-entropy between p and q is

$$H_C[p \| q] = - \sum_{x \in S_X} p[x] \log[q[x]] = H[X] + D_{KL}[p \| q].$$

Cross-entropy can be interpreted as the uncertainty associated with X, where we evaluate its information content using a wrong distribution q rather than the true distribution p. Cross-entropy is a popular scoring function in classification problems, and it is particularly meaningful in financial applications (López de Prado 2018, section 9.4).

3.7 Mutual Information

Mutual information is defined as the decrease in uncertainty (or informational gain) in X that results from knowing the value of Y:

$$I[X,Y] = H[X] - H[X|Y] = H[X] + H[Y] - H[X,Y]$$

$$= \sum_{x \in S_X} \sum_{y \in S_Y} p[x,y] \log\left[\frac{p[x,y]}{p[x]p[y]}\right]$$

$$= D_{KL}[p[x,y] \| p[x]p[y]] = \sum_{y \in S_Y} p[y] \sum_{x \in S_X} p[x|y] \log\left[\frac{p[x|y]}{p[x]}\right]$$

$$= E_Y[D_{KL}[p[x|y] \| p[x]]] = \sum_{x \in S_X} p[x] \sum_{y \in S_Y} p[y|x] \log\left[\frac{p[y|x]}{p[y]}\right]$$

$$= E_X[D_{KL}[p[y|x] \| p[y]]].$$

From the above we can see that $I[X,Y] \geq 0$, $I[X,Y] = I[Y,X]$ and that $I[X,X] = H[X]$. When X and Y are independent, $p[x,y] = p[x]p[y]$, hence $I[X,Y] = 0$. An upper boundary is given by $I[X,Y] \leq \min\{H[X], H[Y]\}$. However, mutual information is *not* a metric, because it does not satisfy the triangle inequality: $I[X,Z] \not\leq I[X,Y] + I[Y,Z]$. An important attribute of mutual information is its grouping property,

$$I[X,Y,Z] = I[X,Y] + I[(X,Y),Z],$$

where (X,Y) represents the joint distribution of X and Y. Since X, Y, and Z can themselves represent joint distributions, the above property can be used to decompose mutual information into simpler constituents. This makes mutual information a useful similarity measure in the context of agglomerative clustering algorithms and forward feature selection.

Given two arrays x and y of equal size, which are discretized into a regular grid with a number of partitions (bins) per dimension, Code Snippet 3.1 shows how to compute in python the marginal entropies, joint entropy, conditional entropies, and the mutual information.

3.8 Variation of Information

Variation of information is defined as

$$VI[X,Y] = H[X|Y] + H[Y|X] = H[X] + H[Y] - 2I[X,Y]$$
$$= 2H[X,Y] - H[X] - H[Y] = H[X,Y] - I[X,Y].$$

This measure can be interpreted as the uncertainty we expect in one variable if we are told the value of other. It has a lower bound in $VI[X,Y] = 0 \Leftrightarrow X = Y$, and an upper

SNIPPET 3.1 MARGINAL, JOINT, CONDITIONAL ENTROPIES, AND MUTUAL INFORMATION

```
import numpy as np,scipy.stats as ss
from sklearn.metrics import mutual_info_score
cXY=np.histogram2d(x,y,bins)[0]
hX=ss.entropy(np.histogram(x,bins)[0]) # marginal
hY=ss.entropy(np.histogram(y,bins)[0]) # marginal
iXY=mutual_info_score(None,None,contingency=cXY)
iXYn=iXY/min(hX,hY) # normalized mutual information
hXY=hX+hY-iXY # joint
hX_Y=hXY-hY # conditional
hY_X=hXY-hX # conditional
```

bound in $VI[X,Y] \leq H[X,Y]$. Variation of information is a metric, because it satisfies the axioms (1) nonnegativity, $VI[X,Y] \geq 0$; (2) symmetry, $VI[X,Y] = VI[Y,X]$; and (3) triangle inequality, $VI[X,Z] \leq VI[X,Y] + VI[Y,Z]$.

Because $H[X,Y]$ is a function of the sizes of S_X and S_Y, $VI[X,Y]$ does not have a firm upper bound. This is problematic when we wish to compare variations of information across different population sizes. The following quantity is a metric bounded between zero and one for all pairs (X,Y):

$$\widetilde{VI}[X,Y] = \frac{VI[X,Y]}{H[X,Y]} = 1 - \frac{I[X,Y]}{H[X,Y]}.$$

Following Kraskov et al. (2008), a sharper alternative bounded metric is

$$\widetilde{\widetilde{VI}}[X,Y] = \frac{\max\{H[X|Y],H[Y|X]\}}{\max\{H[X],H[Y]\}} = 1 - \frac{I[X,Y]}{\max\{H[X],H[Y]\}},$$

where $\widetilde{\widetilde{VI}}[X,Y] \leq \widetilde{VI}[X,Y]$ for all pairs (X,Y). Following the previous example, Code Snippet 3.2 computes mutual information, variation of information, and normalized variation of information.[9]

As a summary, Figure 3.1 provides a visual representation of how these concepts are interrelated.

3.9 Discretization

Throughout this section, we have assumed that random variables were discrete. For the continuous case, we can quantize (coarse-grain) the values, and apply the same concepts on the binned observations. Consider a continuous random variable X, with probability distribution functions $f_X[x]$. Shannon defined its (differential) entropy as

---

[9] Also, see https://pypi.org/project/pyitlib/.

```
import numpy as np,scipy.stats as ss
from sklearn.metrics import mutual_info_score
#-----------------------------------------------------------
def varInfo(x,y,bins,norm=False):
  # variation of information
  cXY=np.histogram2d(x,y,bins)[0]
  iXY=mutual_info_score(None,None,contingency=cXY)
  hX=ss.entropy(np.histogram(x,bins)[0]) # marginal
  hY=ss.entropy(np.histogram(y,bins)[0]) # marginal
  vXY=hX+hY-2*iXY # variation of information
  if norm:
      hXY=hX+hY-iXY # joint
      vXY/=hXY # normalized variation of information
  return vXY
```

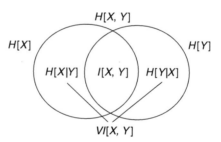

Figure 3.1 Correspondence between joint entropy, marginal entropies, conditional entropies, mutual information, and variation of information.

$$H[X] = - \int_{-\infty}^{\infty} f_X[x]\log[f_X[x]]dx.$$

The entropy of a Gaussian random variable X is $H[X] = 1/2\log[2\pi e\sigma^2]$, thus $H[X] \approx 1.42$ in the standard Normal case. One way to estimate $H[X]$ on a finite sample of real values is to divide the range spanning the observed values $\{x\}$ into B_X bins of equal size Δ_X, $\Delta_X = (\max\{x\} - \min\{x\})/B_X$, giving us

$$H[X] \approx - \sum_{i=1}^{B_X} f_X[x_i]\log[f_X[x_i]]\Delta_X,$$

where $f_X[x_i]$ represents the frequency of observations falling within the ith bin. Let $p[x_i]$ be the probability of drawing an observation within the segment Δ_X

corresponding to the ith bin. We can approximate $p[x_i]$ as $p[x_i] \approx f_X[x_i]\Delta_X$, which can be estimated as $\hat{p}[x_i] = N_i/N$, where N_i is the number of observations within the ith bin, $N = \sum_{i=1}^{B_X} N_i$, and $\sum_{i=1}^{B_X} \hat{p}[x_i] = 1$. This leads to a discretized estimator of entropy of the form

$$\hat{H}[X] = - \sum_{i=1}^{B_X} \frac{N_i}{N} \log \left[\frac{N_i}{N}\right] + \log[\Delta_X].$$

Following the same argument, the estimator of the joint entropy is

$$\hat{H}[X, Y] = - \sum_{i=1}^{B_X} \sum_{j=1}^{B_Y} \frac{N_{i,j}}{N} \log \left[\frac{N_{i,j}}{N}\right] + \log[\Delta_X \Delta_Y].$$

From the estimators $\hat{H}[X]$ and $\hat{H}[X, Y]$, we can derive estimators for conditional entropies, mutual information, and variation of information. As we can see from these equations, results may be biased by our choice of B_X and B_Y. For the marginal entropy case, Hacine-Gharbi et al. (2012) found that the following binning is optimal:

$$B_X = \text{round} \left[\frac{\zeta}{6} + \frac{2}{3\zeta} + \frac{1}{3}\right]$$

$$\zeta = \sqrt[3]{8 + 324N + 12\sqrt{36N + 729N^2}}.$$

For the joint entropy case, Hacine-Gharbi and Ravier (2018) found that the optimal binning is given by

$$B_X = B_Y = \text{round} \left[\frac{1}{\sqrt{2}} \sqrt{1 + \sqrt{1 + \frac{24N}{1 - \hat{\rho}^2}}}\right],$$

where $\hat{\rho}$ is the estimated correlation between X and Y. Code Snippet 3.3 modifies the previous function varInfo, so that it now incorporates the optimal binning derived by function numBins.

3.10 Distance between Two Partitions

In the previous sections, we have derived methods to evaluate the similarity between random variables. We can extend these concepts to the problem of comparing two partitions of the same data set, where the partitions can be considered random to some extent (Meila 2007). A partition P of a data set D is an unordered set of mutually disjoint nonempty subsets:

SNIPPET 3.3 VARIATION OF INFORMATION ON DISCRETIZED CONTINUOUS RANDOM
VARIABLES

```
def numBins(nObs,corr=None):
  # Optimal number of bins for discretization
  if corr is None: # univariate case
    z=(8+324*nObs+12*(36*nObs+729*nObs**2)**.5)**(1/3.)
    b=round(z/6.+2./(3*z)+1./3)
  else: # bivariate case
    b=round(2**-.5*(1+(1+24*nObs/(1.-corr**2))**.5)**.5)
  return int(b)
#-------------------------------------------------------------
def varInfo(x,y,norm=False):
  # variation of information
  bXY=numBins(x.shape[0],corr=np.corrcoef(x,y)[0,1])
  cXY=np.histogram2d(x,y,bXY)[0]
  iXY=mutual_info_score(None,None,contingency=cXY)
  hX=ss.entropy(np.histogram(x,bXY)[0]) # marginal
  hY=ss.entropy(np.histogram(y,bXY)[0]) # marginal
  vXY=hX+hY-2*iXY # variation of information
  if norm:
    hXY=hX+hY-iXY # joint
    vXY/=hXY # normalized variation of information
  return vXY
```

$$P = \{D_k\}_{k=1,\ldots,K},$$

$$\|D_k\| > 0, \forall k,$$

$$D_k \cap D_l = \emptyset, \forall k \neq l,$$

$$\bigcup_{k=1}^{k} D_k = D.$$

Let us define the uncertainty associated with P. First, we set the probability of picking any element $d \in D$ as $\tilde{p}[d] = 1/|D|$. Second, we define the probability that an element $d \in D$ picked at random belongs to subset D_k as $p[k] = |D_k|/|D|$. This second probability $p[k]$ is associated with a discrete random variable that takes a value k from $S = \{1, \ldots, K\}$. Third, the uncertainty associated with this discrete random variable can be expressed in terms of the entropy

$$H[P] = -\sum_{k=1}^{K} p[k]\log[p[k]].$$

From the above we can see that $H[P]$ does not depend on $\|D\|$, but on the relative sizes of the subsets. Given a second partition $P' = \{D'_{k'}\}_{k'=1,...,K'}$, we can define a second random variable that takes a value k' from $S' = \{1, \ldots, K'\}$. The joint probability that an element $d \in D$ picked at random belongs to subset D_k in P and also belongs to subset $D'_{k'}$ in P' is

$$p[k, k'] = \frac{\| D_k \cap D'_{k'} \|}{\|D\|}.$$

The joint entropy is defined as

$$H[P, P'] = -\sum_{k=1}^{K} \sum_{k'=1}^{K'} p[k, k'] \log[p[k, k']],$$

and the conditional entropy is $H[P|P'] = H[P, P'] - H[P]$. The mutual information is

$$I[P, P'] = H[P] - H[P|P'] = \sum_{k=1}^{K} \sum_{k'=1}^{K'} p[k, k'] \log\left[\frac{p[k, k']}{p[k]p[k']}\right],$$

and the variation of information is

$$VI[P, P'] = H[P|P'] + H[P'|P],$$

where $H[P|P']$ measures the amount of information about P that we lose and $H[P'|P]$ measures the amount of information about P' that we gain when going from partition P to P'. This definition of variation of information has several properties, among which we find that (1) it is a metric; (2) it has an absolute upper boundary at $VI[P, P'] \leq \log[\|D\|]$ (like entropy); and (3) if the number of subsets is bounded by a constant $\overline{K}$, with $\overline{K} \leq \sqrt{\|D\|}$, then $VI[P, P'] \leq 2\log[\overline{K}]$. These three properties are important because they allow us to normalize the distance between partitions, and compare partitioning algorithms across different data sets. In the context of unsupervised learning, variation of information is useful for comparing outcomes from a partitional (non-hierarchical) clustering algorithm.

3.11 Experimental Results

The mutual information quantifies the amount of information shared by two random variables. The normalized mutual information takes real values within the range $[0, 1]$, like the absolute value of the correlation coefficient. Also like the correlation coefficient (or its absolute value), neither the mutual information nor the normalized mutual information are true metrics. The mutual information between two random standardized Gaussian variables X and Y with correlation ρ is known to be $I[X, Y] = -1/2\log[1 - \rho^2]$.

It is in this sense that we can consider the normalized mutual information as the information-theoretic analogue to linear algebra's correlation coefficient. Next, we study how both statistics perform under different scenarios.

3.11.1 No Relationship

We begin by drawing two arrays, x and e, of random numbers from a standard Gaussian distribution. Then we compute $y = 0x + e = e$, and evaluate the normalized mutual information as well as the correlation between x and y. Code Snippet 3.4 details these calculations.

SNIPPET 3.4 CORRELATION AND NORMALIZED MUTUAL INFORMATION OF TWO INDEPENDENT GAUSSIAN RANDOM VARIABLES

```
def mutualInfo(x,y,norm=False):
 # mutual information
 bXY=numBins(x.shape[0],corr=np.corrcoef(x,y)[0,1])
 cXY=np.histogram2d(x,y,bXY)[0]
 iXY=mutual_info_score(None,None,contingency=cXY)
 if norm:
     hX=ss.entropy(np.histogram(x,bXY)[0]) # marginal
     hY=ss.entropy(np.histogram(y,bXY)[0]) # marginal
     iXY/=min(hX,hY) # normalized mutual information
 return iXY
#- - - - - - - - - - - - - - - - - - - - - - - - - - - - - - - - - - -
size,seed=5000,0
np.random.seed(seed)
x=np.random.normal(size=size)
e=np.random.normal(size=size)
y=0*x+e
nmi=mutualInfo(x,y,True)
corr=np.corrcoef(x,y)[0,1]
```

Figure 3.2 represents *y* against *x*, which as expected resembles a cloud. Correlation and normalized mutual information are both approximately zero.

3.11.2 Linear Relationship

In this example, we impose a strong linear relationship between x and y, by setting $y = 100x + e$. Now the correlation is approximately 1, and the normalized mutual information is also very high, approximately 0.9. Still, the normalized mutual information is not 1, because there is some degree of uncertainty associated with e. For instance, should we impose $y = 10^4 x + e$, then the normalized mutual information would be 0.995. Figure 3.3 plots this relationship.

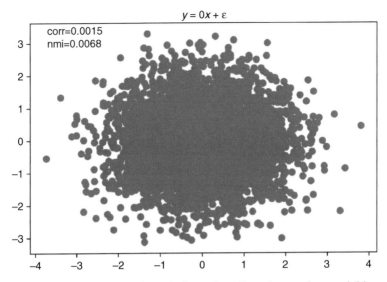

Figure 3.2 Scatterplot of two independent Gaussian random variables.

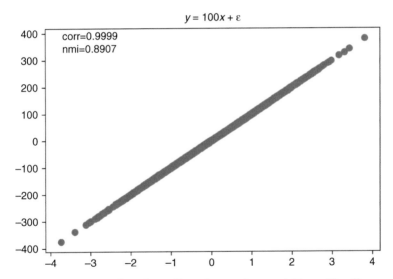

Figure 3.3 Scatterplot of two Gaussian random variables with a linear relationship.

3.11.3 Nonlinear Relationship

In this example, we impose a symmetric relationship across the x-axis between x and y, by setting $y = 100|x| + e$. Now the correlation is approximately 0, and the normalized mutual information is approximately 0.64. As expected, the correlation has failed to recognize the strong relationship that exists between x

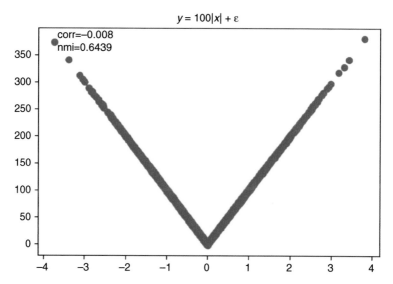

Figure 3.4 Scatterplot of two Gaussian random variables with a nonlinear relationship.

and y, because that relationship is nonlinear. In contrast, the mutual information recognizes that we can extract a substantial amount of information from x that is useful to predict y, and *vice versa*. Figure 3.4 plots this relationship.

Unlike in the linear case, raising the coefficient from 10^2 to 10^4 will not substantially increase the normalized mutual information. In this example, the main source of uncertainty is not e. The normalized mutual information is high, but not 1, because knowing y does not suffice to know x. In fact, there are two alternative values of x associated with each value of y.

3.12 Conclusions

Correlations are useful at quantifying the linear codependency between random variables. This form of codependency accepts various representations as a distance metric, such as $d_\rho[X, Y] = \sqrt{\frac{1}{2}(1 - \rho[X, Y])}$, or $d_{|\rho|}[X, Y] = \sqrt{1 - |\rho[X, Y]|}$. However, when variables X and Y are bound by a nonlinear relationship, the above distance metric misjudges the similarity of these variables. For nonlinear cases, we have argued that the normalized variation of information is a more appropriate distance metric. It allows us to answer questions regarding the unique information contributed by a random variable, without having to make functional assumptions. Given that many ML algorithms do not impose a functional form on the data, it makes sense to use them in conjunction with entropy-based features.

3.13 Exercises

1 Draw 1,000 observations from a bivariate Normal distribution with unit standard deviations and a correlation coefficient $\rho \in \{-1, -.5, 0, .5, 1\}$.

  a Discretize the samples, following the method described in Section 3.9.

  b Compute $H[X], H[Y], H[X, Y], H[X|Y], I[X, Y], VI[X, Y]$ and $\widetilde{VI}[X, Y]$.

  c Are $H[X]$ and $H[Y]$ affected by ρ?

  d Are $H[X, Y], H[X|Y], I[X, Y], VI[X, Y]$, and $\widetilde{VI}[X, Y]$ affected by ρ?

2 Repeat Exercise 1, this time for 1 million observations. What variables are impacted by the different sample size?

3 Repeat Exercise 2, where this time you use the discretization step B_X from Exercise 1. How does this impact the results?

4 What is the main advantage of variation of information over mutual information? Can you think of a use case in finance where mutual information is more appropriate than variation of information?

5 Consider the two correlation-based distance metrics we discussed in Section 3.2. Can you think of a use case where those distance metrics would be preferable to the normalized variation of information?

6 Code in Python a function to compute the KL divergence between two discrete probability distributions.

7 Code in Python a function to compute the cross-entropy of two discrete probability distributions.

8 Prove that $d_{\rho^2}[X, Y] = \sqrt{1 - \rho[X, Y]^2}$ is also a proper metric.

4 Optimal Clustering

4.1 Motivation

A clustering problem consists of a set of objects and a set of features associated with those objects. The goal is to separate the objects into groups (called clusters) using the features, where intragroup similarities are maximized, and intergroup similarities are minimized. It is a form of unsupervised learning, because we do not provide examples to assist the algorithm in solving this task. Clustering problems appear naturally in finance, at every step of the investment process. For instance, analysts may look for historical analogues to current events, a task that involves developing a numerical taxonomy of events. Portfolio managers often cluster securities with respect to a variety of features, to derive relative values among peers. Risk managers are keen to avoid the concentration of risks in securities that share common traits. Traders wish to understand flows affecting a set of securities, to determine whether a rally or sell-off is idiosyncratic to a particular security, or affects a category shared by a multiplicity of securities. In tackling these problems, we use the notions of distance we studied in Section 3. This section focuses on the problem of finding the optimal number and composition of clusters.

4.2 Proximity Matrix

Consider a data matrix X, of order N by F, where N is the number of objects and F is the number of features. We use the F features to compute the proximity between the N objects, as represented by an NxN matrix. The proximity measure can indicate either similarity (e.g., correlation, mutual information) or dissimilarity (e.g., a distance metric). It is convenient but not strictly necessary that dissimilarity measures satisfy the conditions of a metric: nonnegativity, symmetry and triangle inequality (Kraskov et al. 2008). The proximity matrix can be represented as an undirected graph where the weights are a function of the similarity (the more similar, the greater the weight) or dissimilarity (the more dissimilar, the smaller the weight). Then the clustering problem is equivalent to breaking the graph into connected components (disjoint connected subgraphs), one for each cluster. When forming the proximity matrix, it is a good idea to standardize the input data, to prevent that one feature's scale dominates over the rest.

4.3 Types of Clustering

There are two main classes of clustering algorithms: partitional and hierarchical. Partitional techniques create a one-level (un-nested) partitioning of the objects (each object belongs to one cluster, and to one cluster only).

Hierarchical techniques produce a nested sequence of partitions, with a single, all-inclusive cluster at the top and singleton clusters of individual points at the bottom. Hierarchical clustering algorithms can be divisive (top-down) or agglomerative (bottom-up). By restricting the growth of a hierarchical tree, we can derive a partitional clustering from any hierarchical clustering. However, one cannot generally derive a hierarchical clustering from a partitional one.

Depending on the definition of cluster, we can distinguish several types of clustering algorithms, including the following:

1 **Connectivity:** This clustering is based on distance connectivity, like hierarchical clustering. For an example in finance, see López de Prado (2016).
2 **Centroids:** These algorithms perform a vector quantization, like k-means. For an example in finance, see López de Prado and Lewis (2018).
3 **Distribution:** Clusters are formed using statistical distributions, e.g., a mixture of Gaussians.
4 **Density:** These algorithms search for connected dense regions in the data space. Examples include DBSCAN and OPTICS.
5 **Subspace:** Clusters are modeled on two dimensions, features *and* observations. An example is biclustering (also known as coclustering). For instance, they can help identify similarities in subsets of instruments *and* time periods simultaneously.[10]

Some algorithms expect as input a measure of similarity, and other algorithms expect as input a measure of dissimilarity. It is important to make sure that you pass the right input to a particular algorithm. For instance, a hierarchical clustering algorithm typically expects distance as an input, and it will cluster together items within a neighborhood. Centroids, distribution and density methods expect vector-space coordinates, and they can handle distances directly. However, biclustering directly on the distance matrix will cluster together the most distant elements (the opposite of what say k-means would do). One solution is to bicluster on the reciprocal of distance.

If the number of features greatly exceeds the number of observations, the curse of dimensionality can make the clustering problematic: most of the space spanning the observations will be empty, making it difficult to identify any groupings. One solution is to project the data matrix X onto a low-dimensional space, similar to how PCA reduces the number of features (Steinbach et al. 2004; Ding and He 2004). An alternative solution is to project the proximity matrix onto a low-dimensional space, and use it as a new X matrix. In both cases, the procedure described in Section 2 can help identify the number of dimensions associated with signal.

---

[10] For an illustration, see https://quantdare.com/biclustering-time-series/.

4.4 Number of Clusters

Partitioning algorithms find the composition of un-nested clusters, where the researcher is responsible for providing the correct number of clusters. In practice, researchers often do not know in advance what the number of clusters should be. The "elbow method" is a popular technique that stops adding clusters when the marginal percentage of variance explained does not exceed a predefined threshold. In this context, the percentage of variance explained is defined as the ratio of the between-group variance to the total variance (an F-test). One caveat of this approach is that the threshold is often set arbitrarily (Goutte et al. 1999).

In this section we present one algorithm that recovers the number of clusters from a shuffled block-diagonal correlation matrix. López de Prado and Lewis (2018) denote this algorithm ONC, since it searches for the *optimal number of clusters*. ONC belongs to the broader class of algorithms that apply the silhouette method (Rousseeuw 1987). Although we typically focus on finding the number of clusters within a correlation matrix, this algorithm can be applied to any generic observation matrix.

4.4.1 Observations Matrix

If your problem does not involve a correlation matrix, or you already possess an observation matrix, you may skip this section.[11] Otherwise, assume that we have N variables that follow a multivariate Normal distribution characterized by a correlation matrix ρ, where $\rho_{i,j}$ is the correlation between variables i and j. If a strong common component is present, it is advisable to remove it by applying the detoning method explained in Section 2, because a factor exposure shared by all variables may hide the existence of partly shared exposures.

For the purposes of correlation clustering, we can follow at least three approaches: (a) circumvent the X matrix, by directly defining the distance matrix as $d_{i,j} = \sqrt{\frac{1}{2}\left(1 - \rho_{i,j}\right)}$ or a similar transformation (see Section 3); (b) use the correlation matrix as X; (c) derive the X matrix as $X_{i,j} = \sqrt{\frac{1}{2}\left(1 - \rho_{i,j}\right)}$, or a similar transformation (the distance of distances approach). The advantage of options (b) and (c) is that the distance between two variables will be a function of multiple correlation estimates, and not only one, which makes the analysis more robust to the presence of outliers. The advantage of option (c) is

---

[11] Ideally, your observations matrix will be based on one of the information-theoretic metrics explained in Section 3. However, I must concede that correlation is still more prevalent in finance. ONC is agnostic as to how the observations matrix is formed, so the purpose of this section is to explain one way of computing this matrix for readers who feel more comfortable using correlations.

that it acknowledges that a change from $\rho_{i,j} = 0.9$ to $\rho_{i,j} = 1.0$ is greater than a change from $\rho_{i,j} = 0.1$ to $\rho_{i,j} = 0.2$. In this Section we follow approach (c), thus we define the observations matrix as $X_{i,j} = \sqrt{\frac{1}{2}\left(1 - \rho_{i,j}\right)}$.

The clustering of correlation matrices is peculiar in the sense that the features match the observations: we try to group observations where the observations themselves are the features (hence the symmetry of X). Matrix X appears to be a distance matrix, but it is not. It is still an observations matrix, on which distances can be evaluated.

For large matrices X, generally it is good practice to reduce its dimension via PCA. The idea is to replace X with its standardized orthogonal projection onto a lower-dimensional space, where the number of dimensions is given by the number of eigenvalues in X's correlation matrix that exceed λ_+ (see Section 2). The resulting observations matrix, $\widetilde{X}$, of size NxF, has a higher signal-to-noise ratio.

4.4.2 Base Clustering

At this stage, we assume that we have a matrix that expresses our observations in a metric space. This matrix may have been computed as described in the previous section, or applying some other method. For example, the matrix may be based on the variation of information between random variables, as explained in Section 3. Next, let us discuss the base clustering algorithm. One possibility would be to use the k-means algorithm on our observation matrix.[12] While k-means is simple and frequently effective, it does have two notable limitations: first, the algorithm requires an user-set number of clusters K, which is not necessarily optimal a priori; second, the initialization is random, and hence the effectiveness of the algorithm can be similarly random.

In order to address these two concerns, we need to modify the k-means algorithm. The first modification we make is to introduce an objective function, so that we can find the "optimal K." For this, we choose the silhouette score introduced by Rousseeuw (1987). As a reminder, for a given element i and a given clustering, the silhouette coefficient S_i is defined as

$$S_i = \frac{b_i - a_i}{\max\{a_i, b_i\}}; i = 1, \ldots, N,$$

where a_i is the average distance between i and all other elements in the same cluster, and b_i is the average distance between i and all the elements in the

---

[12] Another possibility is to use a hierarchical algorithm, where the base clustering occurs at the dendrogram's distance that maximizes the quality of the partitions. For an example, see https://ssrn.com/abstract=3512998

nearest cluster of which i is not a member. Effectively, this is a measure comparing intracluster distance and intercluster distance. A value $S_i = 1$ means that element i is clustered well, while $S_i = -1$ means that i was clustered poorly. For a given partition, our measure of clustering quality q is defined as

$$q = \frac{E[\{S_i\}]}{\sqrt{V[\{S_i\}]}},$$

where $E[\{S_i\}]$ is the mean of the silhouette coefficients and $V[\{S_i\}]$ is the variance of the silhouette coefficients. The second modification we make deals with k-mean's initialization problem. At the base level, our clustering algorithm performs the following operation: first, evaluate the observation matrix; second, we perform a double for ... loop. In the first loop, we try different $k = 2, \ldots, N$ on which to cluster via k-means for one given initialization, and evaluate the quality q for each clustering. The second loop repeats the first loop multiple times, thereby attempting different initializations. Third, over these two loops, we select the clustering with the highest q. Code Snippet 4.1 implements this procedure, and Figure 4.1 summarizes the workflow.

SNIPPET 4.1 BASE CLUSTERING

```
import numpy as np,pandas as pd
from sklearn.cluster import KMeans
from sklearn.metrics import silhouette_samples
#- - - - - - - - - - - - - - - - - - - - - - - - - - - - - - - - - - - - - -
def clusterKMeansBase(corr0,maxNumClusters=10,n_init=10):
  x,silh=((1-corr0.fillna(0))/2.)**.5,pd.Series() # observations matrix
  for init in range(n_init):
    for i in xrange(2,maxNumClusters+1):
      kmeans_=KMeans(n_clusters=i,n_jobs=1,n_init=1)
      kmeans_=kmeans_.fit(x)
      silh_=silhouette_samples(x,kmeans_.labels_)
      stat=(silh_.mean()/silh_.std(),silh.mean()/silh.std())
      if np.isnan(stat[1]) or stat[0]>stat[1]:
        silh,kmeans=silh_,kmeans_
  newIdx=np.argsort(kmeans.labels_)
  corr1=corr0.iloc[newIdx] # reorder rows

  corr1=corr1.iloc[:,newIdx] # reorder columns
  clstrs={i:corr0.columns[np.where(kmeans.labels_==i)[0]].tolist() \
      for i in np.unique(kmeans.labels_) } # cluster members
  silh=pd.Series(silh,index=x.index)
  return corr1,clstrs,silh
```

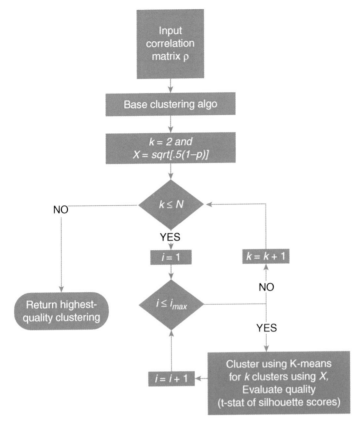

Figure 4.1 Structure of ONC's base clustering stage.

4.4.3 Higher-Level Clustering

Our third modification to k-means deals with clusters of inconsistent quality. The base clustering may capture the more distinct clusters, while missing the less apparent ones. To address this issue, we evaluate the quality q_k of each cluster $k = 1, \ldots, K$ given the clustering quality scores obtained from the base clustering algorithm. We then take the average quality $\bar{q}$, and find the set of clusters with quality below average, $\{q_k | q_k < \bar{q}, k = 1, \ldots, K\}$. Let us denote as K_1 the number of clusters in that set, $K_1 < K$. If the number of clusters to rerun is $K_1 \leq 1$, then we return the clustering given by the base algorithm. However, if $K_1 \geq 2$, we rerun the clustering of the items in those K_1 clusters, while the rest are considered acceptably clustered.

We form a new (reduced) observations matrix out of the elements that compose the K_1 clusters, and rerun the base clustering algorithm on that reduced correlation matrix. Doing so will return a, possibly new, clustering for those elements in K_1. To check its efficacy, we compare the average cluster quality before and after reclustering those elements in K_1. If the average cluster quality improves, we return the accepted clustering from the base clustering concatenated with the new clustering for the redone nodes. Otherwise, we return the clustering formed by the base algorithm. Code Snippet 4.2 implements this operation in python, and Figure 4.2 summarizes the workflow.

SNIPPET 4.2 TOP-LEVEL OF CLUSTERING

```python
from sklearn.metrics import silhouette_samples
#------------------------------------------------------------
def makeNewOutputs(corr0,clstrs,clstrs2):
  clstrsNew={}
  for i in clstrs.keys():
    clstrsNew[len(clstrsNew.keys())]=list(clstrs[i])
  for i in clstrs2.keys():
    clstrsNew[len(clstrsNew.keys())]=list(clstrs2[i])
  newIdx=[j for i in clstrsNew for j in clstrsNew[i]]
  corrNew=corr0.loc[newIdx,newIdx]
  x=((1-corr0.fillna(0))/2.)**.5
  kmeans_labels=np.zeros(len(x.columns))
  for i in clstrsNew.keys():
    idxs=[x.index.get_loc(k) for k in clstrsNew[i]]
    kmeans_labels[idxs]=i
  silhNew=pd.Series(silhouette_samples(x,kmeans_labels),
    index=x.index)
  return corrNew,clstrsNew,silhNew
#------------------------------------------------------------
def clusterKMeansTop(corr0,maxNumClusters=None,n_init=10):
  if maxNumClusters==None:maxNumClusters=corr0.shape[1]-1
  corr1,clstrs,silh=clusterKMeansBase(corr0,maxNumClusters= \
    min(maxNumClusters,corr0.shape[1]-1),n_init=n_init)
  clusterTstats={i:np.mean(silh[clstrs[i]])/ \
    np.std(silh[clstrs[i]]) for i in clstrs.keys()}
  tStatMean=sum(clusterTstats.values())/len(clusterTstats)
  redoClusters=[i for i in clusterTstats.keys() if \
    clusterTstats[i]<tStatMean]
  if len(redoClusters)<=1:
    return corr1,clstrs,silh
  else:
    keysRedo=[j for i in redoClusters for j in clstrs[i]]
    corrTmp=corr0.loc[keysRedo,keysRedo]
    tStatMean=np.mean([clusterTstats[i] for i in redoClusters])
    corr2,clstrs2,silh2=clusterKMeansTop(corrTmp, \
      maxNumClusters=min(maxNumClusters, \
      corrTmp.shape[1]-1),n_init=n_init)
```

```
# Make new outputs, if necessary
corrNew,clstrsNew,silhNew=makeNewOutputs(corr0, \
   {i:clstrs[i] for i in clstrs.keys() if i not in redoClusters}, \
   clstrs2)
newTstatMean=np.mean([np.mean(silhNew[clstrsNew[i]])/ \
   np.std(silhNew[clstrsNew[i]]) for i in clstrsNew.keys()])
if newTstatMean<=tStatMean:
   return corr1,clstrs,silh
else:
   return corrNew,clstrsNew,silhNew
```

4.5 Experimental Results

We now design a Monte Carlo experiment to verify the accuracy of the ONC algorithm introduced earlier: first, we create an NxN correlation matrix ρ from random draws with a predefined number of blocks K, where intrablock correlation is high and across-block correlation is low; second, we shuffle that correlation matrix. Third, we apply ONC, and verify that the ONC algorithm recovers the blocks we injected.[13]

4.5.1 Generation of Random Block Correlation Matrices

Given the tuple (N, M, K), we wish to create a random block correlation matrix of size NxN, made up of K blocks, each of size greater or equal than M. Let us describe the procedure for randomly partitioning N items into K disjoint groups, each of size at least M. Note that this is equivalent to randomly partitioning $N' = N - K(M - 1)$ items into K groups each of size at least 1, so we reduce our analysis to that. Consider randomly choosing $K - 1$ distinct items, denoted as a set B, from the set $A = (1, \ldots, N' - 1)$, then add N' to B, so that B is of size K. Thus, B contains $i_1, \ldots, i_K$, where $1 \leq i_1 < i_2 < \ldots < i_K = N'$. Given B, consider the K partition sets $C_1 = 0, \ldots, i_1 - 1$; $C_2 = i_1, \ldots, i_2 - 1$; $\ldots$; and $C_K = i_{K-1}, \ldots, i_K - 1$. Given that i_j are distinct, each partition contains at least one element as desired, and furthermore completely partitions the set $(0, \ldots, N' - 1)$. In doing so, each set C_j contains $i_j - i_{j-1}$ elements for $j = 1, \ldots, K$, letting $i_0 = 0$. We can generalize again by adding $M - 1$ elements to each block.

Let each block $k = 1, \ldots, K$ have size x_k by x_k, where $x_k \geq M$, thus implying $x_1 + \ldots + x_K = N \geq MK$. First, for each block k, we create a time series of length T that is drawn from independent and identically distributed (IID)

---
[13] I thank Michael J. Lewis for his help in carrying out this experiment.

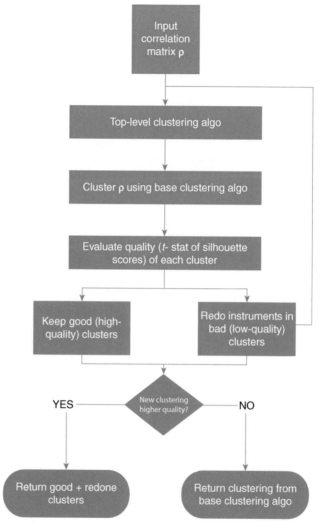

Figure 4.2 Structure of ONC's higher-level stage.

Source: López de Prado and Lewis (2018)

standard Gaussians, then make copies of that to each column of a matrix X of size (T, x_k). Second, we add to each $X_{i,j}$ a random Gaussian noise with standard deviation $\sigma > 0$. By design, the columns of X will be highly correlated for small σ, and less correlated for large σ. Third, we evaluate the covariance matrix Σ_X for the columns of X, and add Σ_X as a block to Σ. Fourth, we add to Σ another covariance matrix with one block but larger σ. Finally, we derive the correlation matrix ρ associated with Σ.

By construction, ρ has K blocks with high correlations inside each block, and low correlations otherwise. Figure 4.3 is an example of a correlation matrix constructed this way. Code Snippet 4.3 implements this operation in python.

SNIPPET 4.3 RANDOM BLOCK CORRELATION MATRIX CREATION

```python
import numpy as np,pandas as pd
from scipy.linalg import block_diag
from sklearn.utils import check_random_state
#---------------------------------------------------
def getCovSub(nObs,nCols,sigma,random_state=None):
  # Sub correl matrix
  rng=check_random_state(random_state)
  if nCols==1:return np.ones((1,1))
  ar0=rng.normal(size=(nObs,1))
  ar0=np.repeat(ar0,nCols,axis=1)
  ar0+=rng.normal(scale=sigma,size=ar0.shape)
  ar0=np.cov(ar0,rowvar=False)
  return ar0
#---------------------------------------------------
def getRndBlockCov(nCols,nBlocks,minBlockSize=1,sigma=1.,
  random_state=None):
  # Generate a block random correlation matrix
  rng=check_random_state(random_state)
  parts=rng.choice(range(1,nCols-(minBlockSize-1)*nBlocks), \
    nBlocks-1,replace=False)
  parts.sort()
  parts=np.append(parts,nCols-(minBlockSize-1)*nBlocks)
  parts=np.append(parts[0],np.diff(parts))-1+minBlockSize
  cov=None
  for nCols_ in parts:
    cov_=getCovSub(int(max(nCols_*(nCols_+1)/2.,100)), \
      nCols_,sigma,random_state=rng)
    if cov is None:cov=cov_.copy()
    else:cov=block_diag(cov,cov_)
  return cov
#---------------------------------------------------
def randomBlockCorr(nCols,nBlocks,random_state=None,
  minBlockSize=1):
  # Form block corr
  rng=check_random_state(random_state)

  cov0=getRndBlockCov(nCols,nBlocks,
    minBlockSize=minBlockSize,sigma=.5,random_state=rng)
  cov1=getRndBlockCov(nCols,1,minBlockSize=minBlockSize,
                  sigma=1.,random_state=rng) # add noise
```

```
cov0+=cov1
corr0=cov2corr(cov0)
corr0=pd.DataFrame(corr0)
return corr0
```

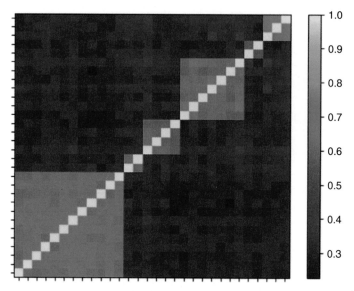

Figure 4.3 Example of a random block correlation matrix, before shuffling.
Source: López de Prado and Lewis (2018)

4.5.2 Number of Clusters

Using the above described procedure, we create random *NxN* correlation matrices with K blocks of size at least M. We shuffle the rows and columns of each correlation matrix, so that the blocks are no longer identifiable. Then, we test the efficacy of the ONC algorithm in recovering the number and composition of those blocks. For our simulations, we chose $N = 20, 40, 80, 160$. As we would expect clusters to be formed of at least two objects, we set $M = 2$, and thus necessarily $K/N \leq 1/2$. For each N, we test $K = 3, 6, \ldots$, up to $N/2$. Finally, we test 1,000 random generations for each of these parameter sets.

Figure 4.4 displays various boxplots for these simulations. In particular, for K/N in a given bucket, we display the boxplot of the ratio of K predicted by the clustering (denoted E[K]) to the actual K tested. Ideally, this ratio should be near 1. Results indicate that ONC frequently recovers the correct number of clusters, with some small errors.

As a reminder, in a boxplot, the central box has the bottom set to the 25th percentile of the data (Q1), while the top is set to the 75th percentile (Q3). The

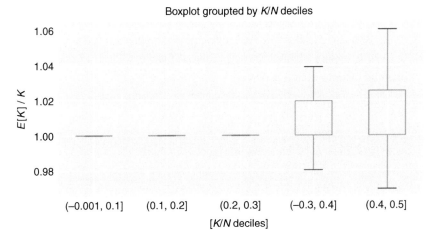

Figure 4.4 Boxplots of estimated K/actual K for bucketed K/N.

Source: López de Prado and Lewis (2018)

interquartile range (IQR) is set to Q3-Q1. The median is displayed as a line inside the box. The "whiskers" extend to the largest datum less than $Q3 + 1.5IQR$, and the smallest datum greater than $Q1–1.5IQR$. Points outside that range are considered outliers.

4.6 Conclusions

In this section, we have studied the problem of determining the optimal composition and number of clusters by a partitioning algorithm. We have made three modifications to the k-means algorithm: (1) we have defined an objective function that measures the quality of the clusters; (2) we have addressed k-mean's initialization problem by rerunning the algorithm with alternative seeds; and (3) an upper-level clustering looks for better partitions among the clusters the exhibit below-average quality. Experimental results show that the algorithm effectively recovers the number and composition of the clusters injected into a block-diagonal matrix.

We have applied the proposed solution to random correlation matrices, however nothing in the method prevents its application to other kinds of matrices. The starting point of the algorithm is an observations matrix, which can be defined in terms of correlation-based metrics, variation of information, or some other function.

4.7 Exercises

1 What is the main difference between outputs from hierarchical and partitioning clustering algorithms? Why can't the output from the latter be converted into the output of the former?

2 Is MSCI's GICS classification system an example of hierarchical or partitioning clustering? Using the appropriate algorithm on a correlation matrix, try to replicate the MSCI classification. To compare the clustering output with MSCI's, use the clustering distance introduced in Section 3.

3 Modify Code Snippets 4.1 and 4.2 to work with a spectral biclustering algorithm. Do you get fundamentally different results? Hint: Remember that, as proximity matrix, biclustering algorithms expect a similarity matrix, not a distance matrix.

4 Repeat the experimental analysis, where this time ONC's base algorithm selects the number of clusters using the "elbow method." Do you recover the true number of clusters consistently? Why?

5 In Section 2, we used a different method for building block-diagonal correlation matrices. In that method, all blocks had the same size. Repeat the experimental analysis on regular block-diagonal correlation matrices. Do you get better or worse results? Why?

5 Financial Labels

5.1 Motivation

Section 4 discussed clustering, a technique that searches for similarities within a data set of features (an X matrix). Clustering is an unsupervised learning method, in the sense that the algorithm does not learn through examples. In contrast, a supervised learning algorithm solves a task with the help of examples (a y array). There are two main types of supervised learning problems: regression and classification. In regression problems, examples are drawn from an infinite population, which can be countable (like integers) or uncountable (like real values). In classification problems, examples are drawn from a finite set of labels (either categorical or ordinal). When there is no intrinsic ordering between the values, labels represent the observations from a categorical variable, like male versus female. When there is intrinsic ordering between the values, labels represent the observations from an ordinal variable, like credit ratings. Real variables can be discretized into categorical or ordinal labels.

Researchers need to ponder very carefully how they define labels, because labels determine the task that the algorithm is going to learn. For example, we may train an algorithm to predict the sign of today's return for stock XYZ, or whether that stock's next 5% move will be positive (a run that spans a variable number of days). The features needed to solve both tasks can be very different, as the first label involves a point forecast whereas the second label relates to a path-dependent event. For example, the sign of a stock's daily return may be unpredictable, while a stock's probability of rallying (unconditional on the time frame) may be assessable. That some features failed to predict one type of label for a particular stock does not mean that they will fail to predict all types of labels for that same stock. Since investors typically do not mind making money one way or another, it is worthwhile to try alternative ways of defining labels. In this section, we discuss four important labeling strategies.

5.2 Fixed-Horizon Method

Virtually all academic studies in financial ML use the fixed-horizon labeling method (see the bibliography). Consider a features matrix X with I rows, $\{X_i\}_{i=1,\dots,I}$, sampled from a series of bars with index $t = 1, \dots, T$, where $I \le T$. We compute the price return over a horizon h as

$$r_{t_{i,0}, t_{i,1}} = \frac{p_{t_{i,1}}}{p_{t_{i,0}}} - 1,$$

where $t_{i,0}$ is the bar index associated with the ith observed features and $t_{i,1} = t_{i,0} + h$ is the bar index after the fixed horizon of h bars has elapsed. This method assigns a label $y_i = \{-1, 0, 1\}$ to an observation X_i, with

$$y_i = \begin{cases} -1 & \text{if } r_{t_{i,0},t_{i,1}} < -\tau, \\ 0 & \text{if } |r_{t_{i,0},t_{i,1}}| \leq \tau, \\ 1 & \text{if } r_{t_{i,0},t_{i,1}} > \tau, \end{cases}$$

where τ is a predefined constant threshold. When the bars are sampled at a regular chronological time frequency, they are known as time bars. Time bars are also very popular in the financial literature. The combination of time bars with fixed-horizon labeling results in fixed time horizons. Despite its popularity, there are several reasons to avoid this method. First, returns computed on time bars exhibit substantial heteroscedasticity, as a consequence of intraday seasonal activity patterns. Applying a constant threshold τ in conjunction with heteroskedastic returns $\{r_{t_{i,0},t_{i,1}}\}_{i=1,\ldots,I}$ will transfer that seasonality to the labels, thus the distribution of labels will not be stationary. For instance, obtaining a 0 label at the open or the close is more informative (in the sense of unexpected) than obtaining a 0 label around noon, or during the night. One solution is to apply the fixed-horizon method on tick, volume or dollar bars (see López de Prado 2018a). Another solution is to label based on standardized returns $z_{t_{i,0},t_{i,1}}$, adjusted for the volatility predicted over the interval of bars $[t_{i,0}, t_{i,1}]$,

$$y_i = \begin{cases} -1 & \text{if } z_{t_{i,0},t_{i,1}} < -\tau, \\ 0 & \text{if } |z_{t_{i,0},t_{i,1}}| \leq \tau, \\ 1 & \text{if } z_{t_{i,0},t_{i,1}} > \tau. \end{cases}$$

A second concern of the fixed horizon method is that it dismisses all information regarding the intermediate returns within the interval $[t_{i,0}, t_{i,1}]$. This is problematic, because positions are typically managed according to profit taking and stop-loss levels. In the particular case of stop losses, those levels may be self-imposed by the portfolio manager, or enforced by the risk department. Accordingly, fixed-horizon labels may not be representative of the outcome of a real investment.

A third concern of the fixed-horizon method is that investors are rarely interested in forecasting whether a return will exceed a threshold τ at a precise point in time $t_{i,0} + h$. It would be more practical to predict the side of the next absolute return that exceeds a threshold τ within a maximum horizon h. The following method deals with these three concerns.

5.3 Triple-Barrier Method

In financial applications, a more realistic method is to make labels reflect the success or failure of a position. A typical trading rule adopted by portfolio managers is to hold a position until the first of three possible outcomes occurs: (1) the unrealized profit target is achieved, and the position is closed with success; (2) the unrealized loss limit is reached, and the position is closed with failure; (3) the position is held beyond a maximum number of bars, and the position is closed without neither failure nor success. In a time plot of position performance, the first two conditions define two horizontal barriers, and the third condition defines a vertical barrier. The index of the bar associated with the first touched barrier is recorded as $t_{i,1}$. When the profit-taking barrier is touched first, we label the observation as $y_i = 1$. When the stop-loss barrier is touched first, we label the observation as $y_i = -1$. When the vertical barrier is touched first, we have two options: we can either label it $y_i = 0$, or we can label it $y_i = \text{sgn}[r_{t_{i,0},t_{i,1}}]$. See López de Prado (2018a) for code snippets that implement the triple-barrier method in python.

Setting profit taking and stop-loss barriers requires knowledge of the position *side* associated with the ith observation. When the position side is unknown, we can still set horizontal barriers as a function of the volatility predicted over the interval of bars $[t_{i,0}, t_{i,0} + h]$, where h is the number of bars until the vertical barrier is touched. In this case, the barriers will be symmetric, because without side information we cannot know which barrier means profit and which barrier means loss.

A key advantage of the triple-barrier method over the fixed-horizon method is that the former incorporates information about the path spanning the interval of bars $[t_{i,0}, t_{i,0} + h]$. In practice, the maximum holding period of an investment opportunity can be defined naturally, and the value of h is not subjective. One disadvantage is that touching a barrier is a discrete event, which may or may not occur by a thin margin. This caveat is addressed by the following method.

5.4 Trend-Scanning Method

In this section we introduce a new labeling method that does not require defining h or profit-taking or stop-loss barriers. The general idea is to identify trends and let them run for as long and as far as they may persist, without setting any barriers.[14] In order to accomplish that, first we need to define what constitutes a trend.

Consider a series of observations $\{x_t\}_{t=1,\dots,T}$, where x_t may represent the price of a security we aim to predict. We wish to assign a label $y_t \in \{-1, 0, 1\}$ to every observation in x_t, based on whether x_t is part of a downtrend, no-trend, or an uptrend. One possibility is to compute the t-value $(\hat{t}_{\hat{\beta}_1})$ associated with the estimated regressor coefficient $(\hat{\beta}_1)$ in a linear time-trend model,

---

[14] The idea of trend scanning is the fruit of joint work with my colleagues Lee Cohn, Michael Lock, and Yaxiong Zeng.

$$x_{t+l} = \beta_0 + \beta_1 l + \varepsilon_{t+l}$$

$$\hat{t}_{\hat{\beta}_1} = \frac{\hat{\beta}_1}{\hat{\sigma}_{\hat{\beta}_1}},$$

where $\hat{\sigma}_{\hat{\beta}_1}$ is the standard error of $\hat{\beta}_1$, and $l = 0, \ldots, L - 1$, and L sets the look-forward period. Code Snippet 5.1 computes this *t*-value on the sample determined by L.

SNIPPET 5.1 *T*-VALUE OF A LINEAR TREND

```
import statsmodels.api as sm1
#-------------------------------------------------------------
def tValLinR(close):
    # tValue from a linear trend
    x=np.ones((close.shape[0],2))
    x[:,1]=np.arange(close.shape[0])
    ols=sm1.OLS(close,x).fit()
    return ols.tvalues[1]
```

Different values of L lead to different *t*-values. To solve this indetermination, we can try a set of alternative values for L, and pick the value of L that maximizes $|\hat{t}_{\hat{\beta}_1}|$. In this way, we label x_t according to the most statistically significant trend observed in the future, out of multiple possible look-forward periods. Code Snippet 5.2 implements this procedure in python. The arguments are molecule, which is the index of observations we wish to label; close, which is the time series of $\{x_t\}$; and span, which is the set of values of L that the algorithm will

---

SNIPPET 5.2 IMPLEMENTATION OF THE TREND-SCANNING METHOD

```
def getBinsFromTrend(molecule,close,span):
    '''
    Derive labels from the sign of t-value of linear trend
    Output includes:
    - t1: End time for the identified trend
    - tVal: t-value associated with the estimated trend coefficient
    - bin: Sign of the trend
    '''
    out=pd.DataFrame(index=molecule,columns=['t1','tVal','bin'])
    hrzns=xrange(*span)
    for dt0 in molecule:
        df0=pd.Series()
        iloc0=close.index.get_loc(dt0)
        if iloc0+max(hrzns)>close.shape[0]:continue
```

```
  for hrzn in hrzns:
     dt1=close.index[iloc0+hrzn-1]
     df1=close.loc[dt0:dt1]
     df0.loc[dt1]=tValLinR(df1.values)
   dt1=df0.replace([-np.inf,np.inf,np.nan],0).abs().idxmax()
   out.loc[dt0,['t1','tVal','bin']]=df0.index[-1],df0[dt1],
     np.sign(df0[dt1]) # prevent leakage
 out['t1']=pd.to_datetime(out['t1'])
 out['bin']=pd.to_numeric(out['bin'],downcast='signed')
 return out.dropna(subset=['bin'])
```

evaluate, in search for the maximum absolute *t*-value. The output is a data frame where the index is the timestamp of the x_t, column t1 reports the timestamp of the farthest observation used to find the most significant trend, column tVal reports the *t*-value associated with the most significant linear trend among the set of evaluated look-forward periods, and column bin is the label (y_t).

Trend-scanning labels are often intuitive, and can be used in classification as well as regression problems. We present an example in the experimental results section.

5.5 Meta-labeling

A common occurrence in finance is that we know whether we want to buy or sell a particular security, however we are less certain about how much we should bet. A model that determines a position's *side* may not be the best one to determine that position's *size*. Perhaps the size should be a function of the recent performance of the model, whereas that recent performance is irrelevant to forecast the position's side.

Having a good bet-sizing model is extremely important. Consider an investment strategy with a precision of 60% and a recall of 90%. A 90% recall means that the strategy predicts ninety out of one hundred true investment opportunities. A 60% precision means that out of one hundred predicted opportunities, sixty are true. Such strategy will lose money if bet sizes are small on the sixty true positives and large on the forty false positives. As investors, we have no (legitimate) control over prices, and the key decision we can and must make is to size bets properly.

Meta-labeling is useful for avoiding or at least reducing an investor's exposure to false positives. It achieves that by giving up some recall in exchange for higher precision. In the example above, adding a meta-labeling layer may result in a recall of 70% and a precision of 70%, hence improving the model's F1-score (the harmonic average of precision and recall). See López de Prado (2018a) for a python implementation of meta-labeling.

The goal of meta-labeling is to train a secondary model on the prediction outcomes of a primary model, where losses are labeled as "0" and gains are labeled as "1." Therefore, the secondary model does not predict the side. Instead, the secondary model predicts whether the primary model will succeed or fail at a particular prediction (a meta-prediction). The probability associated with a "1" prediction can then be used to size the position, as explained next.

5.5.1 Bet Sizing by Expected Sharpe Ratio

Let p be the expected probability that the opportunity yields a profit π, and $1 - p$ the expected probability that the opportunity yields a profit $-\pi$ (i.e., a loss), for some symmetric payoff of magnitude $\pi > 0$. The expected profit from the opportunity is $\mu = p\pi + (1 - p)(-\pi) = \pi(2p - 1)$. The expected variance from the opportunity is $\sigma^2 = 4\pi^2 p(1 - p)$. The Sharpe ratio associated with the opportunity can therefore be estimated as

$$z = \frac{\mu}{\sigma} = \frac{p - \frac{1}{2}}{\sqrt{p(1 - p)}},$$

with $z \in (-\infty, +\infty)$. Assuming that the Sharpe ratio of opportunities follows a standard Gaussian distribution, we may derive the bet size as $m = 2Z[z] - 1$, where $Z[.]$ is the cumulative distribution function of the standard Gaussian, and $m \in [-1, 1]$ follows a uniform distribution.

5.5.2 Ensemble Bet Sizing

Consider n meta-labeling classifiers that make a binary prediction on whether an opportunity will be profitable or not, $y_i = \{0, 1\}$, $i = 1, \ldots, n$. The true probability of being profitable is p, and predictions y_i are drawn from a Bernoulli distribution, so $\sum_{i=1}^{n} y_i \sim B[n, p]$, where $B[n, p]$ is a binomial distribution of n trials with probability p. Assuming that the predictions are independent and identically distributed, the de Moivre–Laplace theorem states that the distribution of $\sum_{i=1}^{n} y_i$ converges to a Gaussian with mean np and variance $np(1 - p)$ as $n \to \infty$. Accordingly, $\lim_{n \to \infty} \frac{1}{n} \sum_{i=1}^{n} y_i \sim N[p, p(1 - p)/n]$, which is a particular case of the Lindeberg–Lévy theorem.

Let us denote as $\hat{p}$ the average prediction across the n meta-labeling classifiers, $\hat{p} = 1/n \sum_{i=1}^{n} y_i$. The standard deviation associated with $\hat{p}$ is $\sqrt{\hat{p}(1 - \hat{p})/n}$. Subject to the null hypothesis $H_0 : p = 1/2$, the statistic $t = (\hat{p} - 1/2)/\sqrt{\hat{p}(1 - \hat{p})}\sqrt{n}$, with $t \in (-\infty, +\infty)$, follows a t-student distribution with $n-1$ degrees of freedom. We may derive the bet size as $m = 2t_{n-1}[t] - 1$, where $t_{n-1}[.]$ is the cumulative distribution function of the t-student with $n-1$ degrees of freedom, and $m \in [-1, 1]$ follows a uniform distribution.

5.6 Experimental Results

In this section, we demonstrate how labels can be generated using the trend-scanning method. Code Snippet 5.3 generates a Gaussian random walk, to which we add a sine trend, to force some inflection points. In that way, we create concave and convex segments that should make the determination of trends more difficult. We then call the getBinsFromTrend function, to retrieve the trend horizons, *t*-values, and labels.

SNIPPET 5.3 TESTING THE TREND-SCANNING LABELING ALGORITHM

```
df0=pd.Series(np.random.normal(0,.1,100)).cumsum()
df0+=np.sin(np.linspace(0,10,df0.shape[0]))
df1=getBinsFromTrend(df0.index,df0,[3,10,1])
mpl.scatter(df1.index,df0.loc[df1.index].values,
  c=df1['bin'].values, cmap='viridis')
mpl.savefig('fig 5.1.png');mpl.clf();mpl.close()
mpl.scatter(df1.index,df0.loc[df1.index].values,c=c,cmap='viridis')
```

Figure 5.1 plots a Gaussian random walk with trend, where the colors differentiate four clearly distinct trends, with 1 labels plotted in yellow and -1 labels

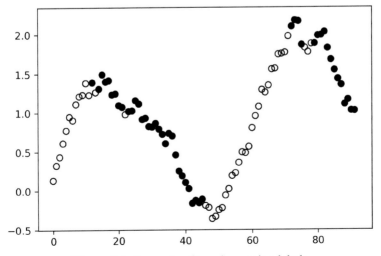

Figure 5.1 Example of trend-scanning labels.

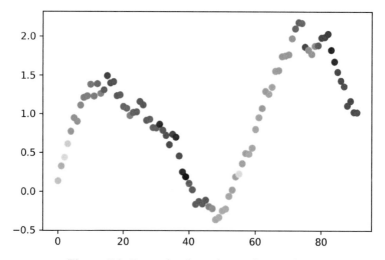

Figure 5.2 Example of trend-scanning *t*-values.

plotted in violet. These binary labels, although appropriate for classification problems, omit information about the strength of the trend.

To correct for that omission, Figure 5.2 plots the same Gaussian random walk with trend, where the colors indicate the magnitude of the *t*-value. Highly positive *t*-values are plotted in yellow, and highly negative *t*-values are plotted in violet. Positive values close to zero are plotted in green, and negative values close to zero are plotted in blue. This information could be used in regression models, or as sample weights in classification problems.

5.7 Conclusions

In this section, we have presented four alternative labeling methods that can be useful in financial applications. The fixed-horizon method, although implemented in most financial studies, suffers from multiple limitations. Among these limitations, we listed that the distribution of fixed-horizon labels may not be stationary, that these labels dismiss path information, and that it would be more practical to predict the side of the next absolute return that exceeds a given threshold.

The triple-barrier method answers these concerns by simulating the outcome of a trading rule. One disadvantage is that touching a barrier is a discrete event, which may or may not occur by a thin margin. To address that, the trend-scanning method determines the side of the strongest linear trend among alternative look-forward periods, with its associated *p*-value. Trend-scanning labels are often intuitive, and can be used in classification as well as regression problems. Finally, the meta-labeling method is useful in applications where the side of a position is predetermined, and we are only interested in learning the size. A proper sizing method can help improve a strategy's performance, by giving up some of the recall in exchange for higher precision.

5.8 Exercises

1 Given a time series of E-mini S&P 500 futures, compute labels on one-minute time bars using the fixed-horizon method, where τ is set at two standard deviations of one-minute returns.

   a Compute the overall distribution of the labels.

   b Compute the distribution of labels across all days, for each hour of the trading session.

   c How different are the distributions in (b) relative to the distribution in (a)? Why?

2 Repeat Exercise 1, where this time you label standardized returns (instead of raw returns), where the standardization is based on mean and variance estimates from a lookback of one hour. Do you reach a different conclusion?

3 Repeat Exercise 1, where this time you apply the triple-barrier method on volume bars. The maximum holding period is the average number of bars per day, and the horizontal barriers are set at two standard deviations of bar returns. How do results compare to the solutions from Exercises 1 and 2?

4 Repeat Exercise 1, where this time you apply the trend-scanning method, with look-forward periods of up to one day. How do results compare to the solutions from Exercises 1, 2, and 3?

5 Using the labels generated in Exercise 3 (triple-barrier method):

   a Fit a random forest classifier on those labels. Use as features estimates of mean return, volatility, skewness, kurtosis, and various differences in moving averages.

   b Backtest those predictions using as a trading rule the same rule used to generate the labels.

   c Apply meta-labeling on the backtest results.

   d Refit the random forest on meta-labels, adding as a feature the label predicted in (a).

   e Size (a) bets according to predictions in (d), and recompute the backtest.

6 Feature Importance Analysis

6.1 Motivation

Imagine that you are given ten puzzles, each of a thousand pieces, where all of the pieces have been shuffled into the same box. You are asked to solve one particular puzzle out of the ten. A reasonable way to proceed is to divide your task into two steps. In the first step, you try to isolate the one thousand pieces that are important to your problem, and discard the nine thousands pieces that are irrelevant. For example, you may notice that about one tenth of the pieces are made of plastic, and the rest are made of paper. Regardless of the pattern shown on the pieces, you know that discarding all paper pieces will isolate a single puzzle. In the second step, you try to fit a structure on the one thousand pieces that you have isolated. Now you may make a guess of what the pattern is, and organize the pieces around it.

Now consider a researcher interested in modeling a dynamic system as a function of many different candidate explanatory variables. Only a small subset of those candidate variables are expected to be relevant, however the researcher does not know in advance which. The approach generally followed in the financial literature is to try to fit a guessed algebraic function on a guessed subset of variables, and see which variables appear to be statistically significant (subject to that guessed algebraic function being correct, including all interaction effects among variables). Such an approach is counterintuitive and likely to miss important variables that would have been revealed by unexplored specifications. Instead, researchers could follow the same steps that they would apply to the problem of solving a puzzle: first, isolate the important variables, irrespective of any functional form, and only then try to fit those variables to a particular specification that is consistent with those isolated variables. ML techniques allow us to disentangle the specification search from the variable search.

In this section, we demonstrate that ML provides intuitive and effective tools for researchers who work on the development of theories. Our exposition runs counter to the popular myth that supervised ML models are black-boxes. According to that view, supervised ML algorithms find predictive patterns, however researchers have no understanding of those findings. In other words, the algorithm has learned something, not the researcher. This criticism is unwarranted.

Even if a supervised ML algorithm does not yield a closed-form algebraic solution (like, for example, a regression method would do), an analysis of its forecasts can tell us what variables are critically involved in a particular phenomenon, what variables are redundant, what variables are useless, and how the relevant variables interact with each other. This kind of analysis is known as "feature importance," and harnessing its power will require us to use everything we have learned in the previous sections.

6.2 *p*-Values

The classical regression framework makes a number of assumptions regarding the fitted model, such as correct model specification, mutually uncorrelated regressors, or white noise residuals. Conditional on those assumptions being true, researchers aim to determine the importance of an explanatory variable through a hypothesis test.[15] A popular way of expressing a variable's significance is through its *p*-value, a concept that dates back to the 1700s (Brian and Jaisson 2007). The *p*-value quantifies the probability that, if the true coefficient associated with that variable is zero, we could have obtained a result equal or more extreme than the one we have estimated. It indicates how incompatible the data are with a specified statistical model. However, a *p*-value does not measure the probability that neither the null nor the alternative hypothesis is true, or that the data are random. And a *p*-value does not measure the size of an effect, or the significance of a result.[16] The misuse of *p*-values is so widespread that the American Statistical Association has discouraged their application going forward as a measure of statistical significance (Wasserstein et al. 2019). This casts a doubt over decades of empirical research in Finance. In order to search for alternatives to the *p*-value, first we must understand its pitfalls.

6.2.1 A Few Caveats of p-Values

A first caveat of *p*-values is that they rely on the strong assumptions outlined earlier. When those assumptions are inaccurate, a *p*-value could be low even though the true value of the coefficient is zero (a false positive), and the *p*-value could be high even though the true value of the coefficient is not zero (a false negative).

A second caveat of *p*-values is that, for highly multicollinear (mutually correlated) explanatory variables, *p*-values cannot be robustly estimated. In multicollinear systems, traditional regression methods cannot discriminate among redundant explanatory variables, leading to substitution effects between related *p*-values.

A third caveat of *p*-values is that they evaluate a probability that is not entirely relevant. Given a null hypothesis H_0 and an estimated coefficient $\hat{\beta}$, the *p*-value estimates the probability of obtaining a result equal or more extreme than $\hat{\beta}$, subject to H_0 being true. However, researchers are often more interested in a different probability, namely, the probability of H_0 being true, subject to having observed $\hat{\beta}$. This probability can be computed using Bayes theorem, alas at the expense of making additional assumptions (Bayesian priors).[17]

---

[15] Some significance tests also demand that the residuals follow a Gaussian distribution.

[16] For additional details, read the "Statement on Statistical Significance and P-Values" by the American Statistical Association (2016) and Wasserstein and Lazar (2016).

[17] We revisit this argument in Section 8.2.

A fourth caveat of *p*-values is that it assesses significance in-sample. The entire sample is used to solve two tasks: estimating the coefficients and determining their significance. Accordingly, *p*-values may be low (i.e., significant) for variables that have no out-of-sample explanatory (i.e., forecasting) value. Running multiple in-sample tests on the same data set is likely to produce a false discovery, a practice known as *p*-hacking.

In summary, *p*-values require that we make many assumptions (caveat #1) in order to produce a noisy estimate (caveat #2) of a probability that we do not really need (caveat #3), and that may not be generalizable out-of-sample (caveat #4). These are not superfluous concerns. In theory, a key advantage of classical methods is that they provide a transparent attribution of significance among explanatory variables. But since that classical attribution has so many caveats in practice, perhaps classical methods could use some help from modern computational techniques that overcome those caveats.

6.2.2 A Numerical Example

Consider a binary random classification problem composed of forty features, where five are informative, thirty are redundant, and five are noise. Code Snippet 6.1 implements function getTestData, which generates informative, redundant, and noisy features. Informative features (marked with the "I_" prefix) are those used to generate labels. Redundant features (marked with the "R_" prefix) are those that are formed by adding Gaussian noise to a randomly chosen informative feature (the lower the value of sigmaStd, the greater the substitution effect). Noise features (marked with the "N_" prefix) are those that are not used to generate labels.

Figure 6.1 plots the *p*-values that result from a logit regression on those features. The horizontal bars report the *p*-values, and the vertical dashed line marks the 5% significance level. Only four out of the thirty-five nonnoise features are deemed statistically significant: I_1, R_29, R_27, I_3. Noise features are ranked as relatively important (with positions 9, 11, 14, 18, and 26). Fourteen of the features ranked as least important are not noise. In short, these *p*-values misrepresent the ground truth, for the reasons explained earlier.

Unfortunately, financial data sets tend to be highly multicollinear, as a result of common risk factors shared by large portions of the investment universe: market, sector, rating, value, momentum, quality, duration, etc. Under these circumstances, financial researchers should cease to rely exclusively on *p*-values. It is important for financial researchers to become familiar with additional methods to determine what variables contain information in a particular phenomenon.

SNIPPET 6.1 GENERATING A SET OF INFORMED, REDUNDANT, AND NOISE EXPLANATORY VARIABLES

```
def getTestData (n_features=100,n_informative=25,n_redundant=25,
  n_samples=10000,random_state=0,sigmaStd=.0):
  # generate a random dataset for a classification problem
  from sklearn.datasets import make_classification
  np.random.seed(random_state)
  X,y=make_classification(n_samples=n_samples,
    n_features=n_features-n_redundant,
    n_informative=n_informative,n_redundant=0,shuffle=False,
    random_state=random_state)
  cols=['I_'+str(i) for i in xrange(n_informative)]
  cols+=['N_'+str(i) for i in xrange(n_features-n_informative- \
    n_redundant)]
  X,y=pd.DataFrame(X,columns=cols),pd.Series(y)
  i=np.random.choice(xrange(n_informative),size=n_redundant)
  for k,j in enumerate(i):
    X['R_'+str(k)]=X['I_'+str(j)]+np.random.normal(size= \
      X.shape[0])*sigmaStd
  return X,y
#- - - - - - - - - - - - - - - - - - - - - - - - - - - - - - - - - -
import numpy as np,pandas as pd,seaborn as sns
import statsmodels.discrete.discrete_model as sm
X,y=getTestData(40,5,30,10000,sigmaStd=.1)
ols=sm.Logit(y,X).fit()
```

6.3 Feature Importance

In this section, we study how two of ML's feature importance methods address the caveats of *p*-values, with minimal assumptions, using computational techniques. Other examples of ML interpretability methods are accumulated local effects (Apley 2016) and Shapley values (Štrumbelj 2014).

6.3.1 Mean-Decrease Impurity

Suppose that you have a learning sample of size N, composed of F features, $\{X_f\}_{f=1,...,F}$ and one label per observation. A tree-based classification (or regression) algorithm splits at each node t its labels into two samples: for a given feature X_f, labels in node t associated with a X_f below a threshold τ are placed in the left sample, and the rest are placed in the right sample. For each of these samples, we can evaluate their impurity as the entropy of the distribution of labels, as the Gini index, or following some other criterion. Intuitively, a sample is purest when it contains only labels of one kind, and it is most impure

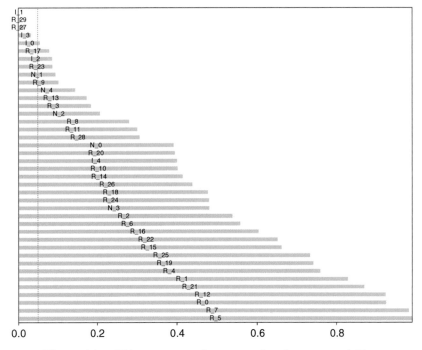

Figure 6.1 *p*-Values computed on a set of explanatory variables.

when its labels follow a uniform distribution. The information gain that results from a split is measured in terms of the resulting reduction in impurity,

$$\Delta g[t,f] = i[t] - \frac{N_t^{(0)}}{N_t} i[t^{(0)}] - \frac{N_t^{(1)}}{N_t} i[t^{(1)}],$$

where $i[t]$ is the impurity of labels at node t (before the split), $i[t^{(0)}]$ is the impurity of labels in the left sample, and $i[t^{(1)}]$ is the impurity of labels in the right sample. At each node t, the classification algorithm evaluates $\Delta g[t,f]$ for various features in $\{X_f\}_{f=1,\ldots,F}$, determines the optimal threshold τ that maximizes $\Delta g[t,f]$ for each of them, and selects the feature f associated with greatest $\Delta g[t,f]$. The classification algorithm continues splitting the samples further until no additional information gains can be produced, or some early-stopping condition is met, such as achieving an impurity below the maximum acceptable limit.

The importance of a feature can be computed as the weighted information gain ($\Delta g[t,f]$) across all nodes where that feature was selected. This tree-based feature importance concept, introduced by Breiman (2001), is known as mean-decrease impurity (MDI). By construction, the MDI value associated with each feature is bounded between 0 and 1, and all combined add up to 1. In the presence of F features where all are uninformative (or equally informed), each MDI value is expected to be $1/F$. For algorithms that combine ensembles of trees, like random forests, we can further estimate the mean and variance of MDI values for each feature across all trees. These mean and variance estimates, along with the central limit theorem, are useful in testing the significance of a feature against a user-defined null hypothesis. Code Snippet 6.2 implements an ensemble MDI procedure. See López de Prado (2018a) for practical advice on how to use MDI.

SNIPPET 6.2 IMPLEMENTATION OF AN ENSEMBLE MDI METHOD

```
def featImpMDI(fit,featNames):
  # feat importance based on IS mean impurity reduction
  df0={i:tree.feature_importances_ for i,tree in \
    enumerate(fit.estimators_)}
  df0=pd.DataFrame.from_dict(df0,orient='index')
  df0.columns=featNames
  df0=df0.replace(0,np.nan) #because max_features=1
  imp=pd.concat({'mean':df0.mean(),
    'std':df0.std()*df0.shape[0]**-.5},axis=1) # CLT
  imp/=imp['mean'].sum()
  return imp
#- - - - - - - - - - - - - - - - - - - - - - - - - - - - - - - - - - - - - -
from sklearn.tree import DecisionTreeClassifier
from sklearn.ensemble import BaggingClassifier
X,y=getTestData(40,5,30,10000,sigmaStd=.1)
clf=DecisionTreeClassifier(criterion='entropy',max_features=1,
  class_weight='balanced',min_weight_fraction_leaf=0)
clf=BaggingClassifier(base_estimator=clf,n_estimators=1000,
  max_features=1.,max_samples=1.,oob_score=False)
fit=clf.fit(X,y)
imp=featImpMDI(fit,featNames=X.columns)
```

Figure 6.2 plots the result of applying MDI to the same random classification problem discussed in Figure 6.1. The horizontal bars indicate the mean of MDI values across 1,000 trees in a random forest, and the lines indicate the standard deviation around that mean. The more trees we add to the forest, the smaller becomes the standard deviation around the mean. MDI does a good job, in the sense that all of the nonnoisy features (either informed or redundant) are ranked higher than the noise features. Still, a small number of nonnoisy features appear to be much more important than their peers. This is the kind of substitution effects that we anticipated to find in the presence of redundant features. Section 6.5 proposes a solution to this particular concern.

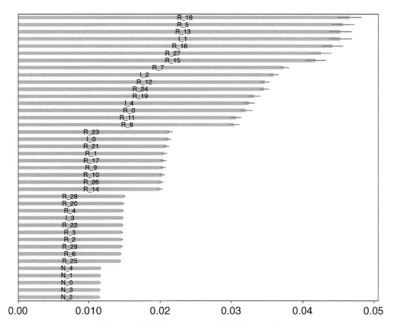

Figure 6.2 Example of MDI results.

Out of the four caveats of p-values, the MDI method deals with three: (1) MDI's computational nature circumvents the need for strong distributional assumptions that could be false (caveat #1) – we are not imposing a particular tree structure or algebraic specification, or relying on stochastic or distributional characteristics of residuals. (2) Whereas betas are estimated on a single sample, ensemble MDIs are derived from a bootstrap of trees. Accordingly, the variance of MDI estimates can be reduced by increasing the number of trees in ensemble methods in general, or in a random forest in particular (caveat 2). This reduces the probability of false positives caused by overfitting. Also, unlike p-values, MDI's estimation does not require the inversion of a possibly ill-conditioned matrix. (3) The goal of the tree-based classifiers is not to estimate the coefficients of a given algebraic equation, thus estimating the probability of a particular null hypothesis is irrelevant. In other words, MDI corrects for caveat 3 by finding the important features in general, irrespective of any particular parametric specification.

An ensemble estimate of MDI will exhibit low variance given a sufficient number of trees, hence reducing the concern of p-hacking. But still, the procedure itself does not involve cross-validation. Therefore, the one caveat of p-values that MDI does not fully solve is that MDI is also computed in-sample (caveat #4). To confront this final caveat, we need to introduce the concept of mean-decrease accuracy.

6.3.2 Mean-Decrease Accuracy

A disadvantage of both *p*-values and MDI is that a variable that appears to be significant for explanatory purposes (in-sample) may be irrelevant for forecasting purposes (out-of-sample). To solve this problem (caveat #4), Breiman (2001) introduced the mean-decrease accuracy (MDA) method.[18] MDA works as follows: first, it fits a model and computes its cross-validated performance; second, it computes the cross-validated performance of the same fitted model, with the only difference that it shuffles the observations associated with one of the features. That gives us one modified cross-validated performance per feature. Third, it derives the MDA associated with a particular feature by comparing the cross-validated performance before and after shuffling. If the feature is important, there should be a significant decay in performance caused by the shuffling, as long as the features are independent. An important attribute of MDA is that, like ensemble MDIs, it is not the result of a single estimate, but rather the average of multiple estimates (one for each testing set in a k-fold cross-validation).

When features are not independent, MDA may underestimate the importance of interrelated features. At the extreme, given two highly important but identical features, MDA may conclude that both features are relatively unimportant, because the effect of shuffling one may be partially compensated by not shuffling the other. We address this concern in Section 6.5.

MDA values are not bounded, and shuffling a feature could potentially improve the cross-validated performance, when the feature is uninformative to the point of being detrimental. Because MDA involves a cross-validation step, this method can be computationally expensive. Code Snippet 6.3 implements MDA. See López de Prado (2018a) for practical advice on how to use MDA.

Figure 6.3 plots the result of applying MDA to the same random classification problem we discussed in Figure 6.2. We can draw similar conclusions as we did in the MDI example. First, MDA does a good job overall at separating noise features from the rest. Noise features are ranked last. Second, noise features are also deemed unimportant in magnitude, with MDA values of essentially zero. Third, although substitution effects contribute to higher variances in MDA importance, none is high enough to question the importance of the nonnoisy features.

Despite its name, MDA does not necessarily rely on accuracy to evaluate the cross-validated performance. MDA can be computed on other performance scores. In fact, in the particular case of finance, accuracy is not a particularly good choice. The reason is, accuracy scores a classifier in terms of its proportion of correct predictions. This has the disadvantage that probabilities are not taken into account.

---

[18] This is sometimes also known as permutation importance.

SNIPPET 6.3 IMPLEMENTATION OF MDA

```
def featImpMDA(clf,X,y,n_splits=10):
  # feat importance based on OOS score reduction
  from sklearn.metrics import log_loss
  from sklearn.model_selection._split import KFold
  cvGen=KFold(n_splits=n_splits)
  scr0,scr1=pd.Series(),pd.DataFrame(columns=X.columns)
  for i,(train,test) in enumerate(cvGen.split(X=X)):
    X0,y0=X.iloc[train,:],y.iloc[train]
    X1,y1=X.iloc[test,:],y.iloc[test]
    fit=clf.fit(X=X0,y=y0) # the fit occurs here
    prob=fit.predict_proba(X1) # prediction before shuffling
    scr0.loc[i]=-log_loss(y1,prob,labels=clf.classes_)
    for j in X.columns:
      X1_=X1.copy(deep=True)
      np.random.shuffle(X1_[j].values) # shuffle one column
      prob=fit.predict_proba(X1_) # prediction after shuffling
      scr1.loc[i,j]=-log_loss(y1,prob,labels=clf.classes_)
  imp=(-1*scr1).add(scr0,axis=0)
  imp=imp/(-1*scr1)
  imp=pd.concat({'mean':imp.mean(),
    'std':imp.std()*imp.shape[0]**-.5},axis=1) # CLT
  return imp
#- - - - - - - - - - - - - - - - - - - - - - - - - - - - - - - - - - - - - - - -
X,y=getTestData(40,5,30,10000,sigmaStd=.1)
clf=DecisionTreeClassifier(criterion='entropy',max_features=1,
  class_weight='balanced',min_weight_fraction_leaf=0)
clf=BaggingClassifier(base_estimator=clf,n_estimators=1000,
  max_features=1.,max_samples=1.,oob_score=False)
imp=featImpMDA(clf,X,y,10)
```

For example, a classifier may achieve high accuracy even though it made good predictions with low confidence and bad predictions with high confidence. In the following section, we introduce a scoring function that addresses this concern.

6.4 Probability-Weighted Accuracy

In financial applications, a good alternative to accuracy is log-loss (also known as cross-entropy loss). Log-loss scores a classifier in terms of the average log-likelihood of the true labels (for a formal definition, see section 9.4 of López de Prado 2018a). One disadvantage, however, is that log-loss scores are not easy to interpret and compare. A possible solution is to compute the negative average likelihood of the true labels (NegAL),

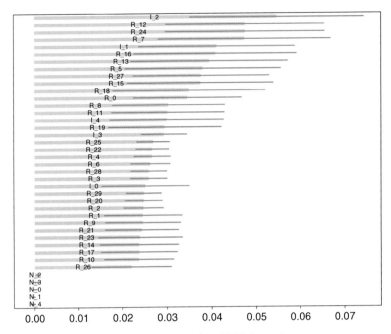

Figure 6.3 Example of MDA results.

$$\text{NegAL} = -N^{-1}\sum_{n=0}^{N-1}\sum_{k=0}^{K-1}y_{n,k}p_{n,k},$$

where $p_{n,k}$ is the probability associated with prediction n of label k and $y_{n,k}$ is an indicator function, $y_{n,k} \in \{0,1\}$, where $y_{n,k} = 1$ when observation n was assigned label k and $y_{n,k} = 0$ otherwise. This is very similar to log-loss, with the difference that it averages likelihoods rather than log-likelihoods, so that NegAL still ranges between 0 and 1.

Alternatively, we can define the probability-weighted accuracy (PWA) as

$$\text{PWA} = \sum_{n=0}^{N-1}y_n\left(p_n - K^{-1}\right) \bigg/ \sum_{n=0}^{N-1}\left(p_n - K^{-1}\right),$$

where $p_n = \max_k\{p_{n,k}\}$ and y_n is an indicator function, $y_n \in \{0,1\}$, where $y_n = 1$ when the prediction was correct, and $y_n = 0$ otherwise.[19] This is equivalent to standard accuracy when the classifier has absolute conviction in every prediction ($p_n = 1$ for all n). PWA punishes bad predictions made with high confidence more severely than accuracy, but less severely than log-loss.

---

[19] The idea of PWA is the fruit of joint work with my colleagues Lee Cohn, Michael Lock, and Yaxiong Zeng.

6.5 Substitution Effects

Substitution effects arise when two features share predictive information. Substitution effects can bias the results from feature importance methods. In the case of MDI, the importance of two identical features will be halved, as they are randomly chosen with equal probability. In the case of MDA, two identical features may be considered relatively unimportant, even if they are critical, because the effect of shuffling one may be compensated by the other.

6.5.1 Orthogonalization

When features are highly codependent, their importance cannot be adjudicated in a robust manner. Small changes in the observations may have a dramatic impact on their estimated importance. However, this impact is not random: given two highly codependent features, the drop in importance from one is compensated with the raise in importance of the other. In other words, code-pendence causes substitution effects when evaluating the importance of features.

One solution to multicollinearity is to apply PCA on the features, derive their orthogonal principal components, and then run MDI or MDA on those principal components (for additional details, see chapter 8 of López de Prado 2018a). Features orthogonalized in this way may be more resilient to substitution effects, with three caveats: (1) redundant features that result from nonlinear combinations of informative ones will still cause substitution effects; (2) the principal components may not have an intuitive explanation; (3) the principal components are defined by eigen-vectors that do not necessarily maximize the model's out-of-sample performance (Witten et al. 2013).

6.5.2 Cluster Feature Importance

A better approach, which does not require a change of basis, is to cluster similar features and apply the feature importance analysis at the cluster level. By construction, clusters are mutually dissimilar, hence taming the substitution effects. Because the analysis is done on a partition of the features, without a change of basis, results are usually intuitive.

Let us introduce one algorithm that implements this idea. The clustered feature importance (CFI) algorithm involves two steps: (1) finding the number and constituents of the clusters of features; (2) applying the feature importance analysis on groups of similar features rather than on individual features.

Step 1: Features Clustering

First, we project the observed features into a metric space, resulting in a matrix $\{X_f\}_{f=1,\ldots,F}$. To form this matrix, one possibility is to follow the correlation-based approach described in Section 4.4.1. Another possibility is to apply information-theoretic concepts (such as variation of information; see Section 3) to represent those features in a metric space. Information-theoretic metrics have the advantage of recognizing redundant features that are the result of nonlinear combinations of informative features.[20]

Second, we apply a procedure to determine the optimal number and composition of clusters, such as the ONC algorithm (see Section 4). Remember that ONC finds the optimal number of clusters as well as the composition of those clusters, where each feature belongs to one and only one cluster. Features that belong to the same cluster share a large amount of information, and features that belong to different clusters share only a relatively small amount of information.

Some silhouette scores may be low due one feature being a combination of multiple features across clusters. This is a problem, because ONC cannot assign one feature to multiple clusters. In this case, the following transformation may help reduce the multicollinearity of the system. For each cluster $k = 1, \ldots, K$, replace the features included in that cluster with residual features, where those residual features do not contain information from features *outside* cluster k. To be precise, let D_k be the subset of index features $D = \{1, \ldots, F\}$ included in cluster k, where $D_k \subset D$, $\| D_k \| > 0, \forall\ k$; $D_k \cap D_l = \varnothing, \forall k \neq l$; $U_{k=1}^{K} D_k = D$. Then, for a given feature X_i where $i \in D_k$, we compute the residual feature $\hat{\varepsilon}_i$ by fitting

$$X_{n,i} = \alpha_i + \sum_{j \in \left\{ U_{l<k} D_l \right\}} \beta_{i,j} X_{n,j} + \varepsilon_{n,i}$$

where $n = 1, \ldots, N$ is the index of observations per feature. If the degrees of freedom in the above regression is too low, one option is to use as regressors linear combinations of the features within each cluster (e.g., following a minimum variance weighting scheme), so that only $K - 1$ betas need to be estimated. One of the properties of OLS residuals is that they are orthogonal to the regressors. Thus, by replacing each feature X_i with its residual equivalent $\hat{\varepsilon}_i$, we remove from cluster k information that is already included in other clusters, while preserving the information that exclusively belongs to cluster k. Again, this transformation is not necessary if the silhouette scores clearly indicate that features belong to their respective clusters.

---

[20] For an example of features clustering with an information-theoretic distance metric, see https://ssrn.com/abstract=3517595

Step 2: Clustered Importance

Step 1 has identified the number and composition of the clusters of features. We can use this information to apply MDI and MDA on groups of similar features, rather than on individual features. In the following, we assume that a partitional algorithm has clustered the features, however this notion of clustered feature importance can be applied to hierarchical clusters as well.

Clustered MDI

As we saw in Section 6.3.1, the MDI of a feature is the weighted impurity reduction across all nodes where that feature was selected. We compute the clustered MDI as the sum of the MDI values of the features that constitute that cluster. If there is one feature per cluster, then MDI and clustered MDI are the same. In the case of an ensemble of trees, there is one clustered MDI for each tree, which allows us to compute the mean clustered MDI, and standard deviation around the mean clustered MDI, similarly to how we did for the feature MDI. Code Snippet 6.4 implements the procedure that estimates the clustered MDI.

```
SNIPPET 6.4 CLUSTERED MDI
def groupMeanStd(df0,clstrs):
  out=pd.DataFrame(columns=['mean','std'])
  for i,j in clstrs.iteritems():
    df1=df0[j].sum(axis=1)
    out.loc['C_'+str(i),'mean']=df1.mean()
    out.loc['C_'+str(i),'std']=df1.std()*df1.shape[0]**-.5
  return out
#- - - - - - - - - - - - - - - - - - - - - - - - - - - - - - - - - - - - - - -
def featImpMDI_Clustered(fit,featNames,clstrs):
  df0={i:tree.feature_importances_ for i,tree in \
    enumerate(fit.estimators_)}
  df0=pd.DataFrame.from_dict(df0,orient='index')
  df0.columns=featNames
  df0=df0.replace(0,np.nan) # because max_features=1
  imp=groupMeanStd(df0,clstrs)
  imp/=imp['mean'].sum()
  return imp
```

Clustered MDA

The MDA of a feature is computed by comparing the performance of an algorithm before and after shuffling that feature. When computing clustered MDA, instead of shuffling one feature at a time, we shuffle all of the features that constitute a given cluster. If there is one cluster per feature, then MDA and clustered MDA are the

SNIPPET 6.5 CLUSTERED MDA

```
def featImpMDA_Clustered(clf,X,y,clstrs,n_splits=10):
  from sklearn.metrics import log_loss
  from sklearn.model_selection._split import KFold
  cvGen=KFold(n_splits=n_splits)
  scr0,scr1=pd.Series(),pd.DataFrame(columns=clstrs.keys())
  for i,(train,test) in enumerate(cvGen.split(X=X)):
    X0,y0=X.iloc[train,:],y.iloc[train]
    X1,y1=X.iloc[test,:],y.iloc[test]
    fit=clf.fit(X=X0,y=y0)
    prob=fit.predict_proba(X1)
    scr0.loc[i]=-log_loss(y1,prob,labels=clf.classes_)
    for j in scr1.columns:
      X1_=X1.copy(deep=True)
      for k in clstrs[j]:
        np.random.shuffle(X1_[k].values) # shuffle cluster
      prob=fit.predict_proba(X1_)
      scr1.loc[i,j]=-log_loss(y1,prob,labels=clf.classes_)
  imp=(-1*scr1).add(scr0,axis=0)
  imp=imp/(-1*scr1)
  imp=pd.concat({'mean':imp.mean(),
    'std':imp.std()*imp.shape[0]**-.5},axis=1)
  imp.index=['C_'+str(i) for i in imp.index]
  return imp
```

same. Code Snippet 6.5 implements the procedure that estimates the clustered MDA.

6.6 Experimental Results

In this experiment we are going to test the clustered MDI and MDA procedures on the same data set we used on the nonclustered versions of MDI and MDA (see Sections 6.3.1 and 6.3.2). That data set consisted of forty features, of which five were informative, thirty were redundant, and five were noise. First, we apply the ONC algorithm to the correlation matrix of those features.[21] In a nonexperimental setting, the researcher should denoise and detone the correlation matrix before clustering, as explained in Section 2. We do not do so in this experiment as a matter of testing the robustness of the method (results are expected to be better on a denoised and detoned correlation matrix).

---

[21] As an exercise, we ask the reader to apply ONC on a metric projection of the features computed using the normalized variation of information.

Figure 6.4 shows that ONC correctly recognizes that there are six relevant clusters (one cluster for each informative feature, plus one cluster of noise features), and it assigns the redundant features to the cluster that contains the informative feature from which the redundant features were derived. Given the low correlation across clusters, there is no need to replace the features with their residuals (as proposed in Section 6.5.2.1). Code Snippet 6.6 implements this example.

SNIPPET 6.6 FEATURES CLUSTERING STEP

```
X,y=getTestData(40,5,30,10000,sigmaStd=.1)
corr0,clstrs,silh=clusterKMeansBase(X.corr(),maxNumClusters=10,
    n_init=10)
sns.heatmap(corr0,cmap='viridis')
```

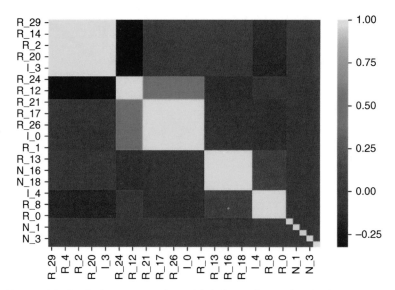

Figure 6.4 ONC clusters together with informative and redundant features.

Next, we apply our clustered MDI method on that data set. Figure 6.5 shows the clustered MDI output, which we can compare with the unclustered output reported in Figure 6.2. The "C_" prefix indicates the cluster, and "C_5" is the cluster associated with the noise features. Clustered features "C_1" is the second least important, however its importance is more than double the importance of "C_5." This is in contrast with what we saw in Figure 6.2, where there was a small difference in importance between the noise features and some of the nonnoisy features. Thus, the clustered MDI method appears to work better than the standard MDI method. Code Snippet 6.7 shows how these results were computed.

SNIPPET 6.7 CALLING THE FUNCTIONS FOR CLUSTERED MDI

```
clf=DecisionTreeClassifier(criterion='entropy',max_features=1,
   class_weight='balanced',min_weight_fraction_leaf=0)
clf=BaggingClassifier(base_estimator=clf,n_estimators=1000,
   max_features=1.,max_samples=1.,oob_score=False)
fit=clf.fit(X,y)
imp=featImpMDI_Clustered(fit,X.columns,clstrs)
```

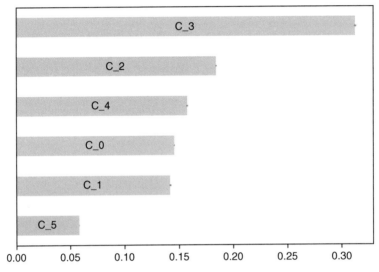

Figure 6.5 Clustered MDI.

Finally, we apply our clustered MDA method on that data set. Figure 6.6 shows the clustered MDA output, which we can compare with the unclustered output reported in Figure 6.3. Again, "C_5" is the cluster associated with the noise features, and all other clusters are associated with informative and redundant features. This analysis has reached two correct conclusions: (1) "C_5" has essentially zero importance, and should be discarded as irrelevant; and (2) all other clusters have very similar importance. This is in contrast with what we saw in Figure 6.3, where some nonnoise features appeared to be much more important than others, even after taking into consideration the standard derivation around the mean values. Code Snippet 6.8 shows how these results were computed.

6.7 Conclusions

Most researchers use *p*-values to evaluate the significance of explanatory variables. However, as we saw in this section, *p*-values suffer from four major flaws. ML offers feature importance methods that overcome most or all of those flaws.

SNIPPET 6.8 CALLING THE FUNCTIONS FOR CLUSTERED MDA

```
clf=DecisionTreeClassifier(criterion='entropy',max_features=1,
    class_weight='balanced',min_weight_fraction_leaf=0)
clf=BaggingClassifier(base_estimator=clf,n_estimators=1000,
    max_features=1.,max_samples=1.,oob_score=False)
imp=featImpMDA_Clustered(clf,X,y,clstrs,10)
```

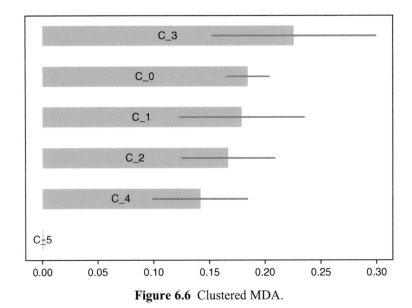

Figure 6.6 Clustered MDA.

The MDI and MDA methods assess the importance of features robustly and without making strong assumptions about the distribution and structure of the data. Unlike *p*-values, MDA evaluates feature importance in cross-validated experiments. Furthermore, unlike *p*-values, clustered MDI and clustered MDA estimates effectively control for substitution effects. But perhaps the most salient advantage of MDI and MDA is that, unlike classical significance analyses, these ML techniques evaluate the importance of a feature irrespective of any particular specification. In doing so, they provide information that is extremely useful for the development of a theory. Once the researcher knows the variables involved in a phenomenon, she can focus her attention on finding the mechanism or specification that binds them together.

The implication is that classical statistical approaches, such as regression analysis, are not necessarily more transparent or insightful than their ML counterparts. The perception that ML tools are black-boxes and classical tools are white-boxes is false. Not only can ML feature importance methods be as helpful as *p*-values, but in some cases they can be more insightful and accurate.

A final piece of advice is to consider carefully what are we interested in explaining or predicting. In Section 5, we reviewed various labeling methods. The same features can yield various degrees of importance in explaining or predicting different types of labels. Whenever possible, it makes sense to apply these feature importance methods to all of the labeling methods discussed earlier, and see what combination of features and labels leads to the strongest theory. For instance, you may be indifferent between predicting the sign of the next trend or predicting the sign of the next 5% return, because you can build profitable strategies on either kind of prediction (as long as the feature importance analysis suggests the existence of a strong theoretical connection).

6.8 Exercises

1 Consider a medical test with a false positive rate $\alpha = P[x > \tau|H_0]$, where H_0 is the null hypothesis (the patient is healthy), x is the observed measurement, and τ is the significance threshold. A test is run on a random patient and comes back positive (the null hypothesis is rejected). What is the probability that the patient truly has the condition?

   a Is it $1 - \alpha = P[x \le \tau|H_0]$ (the confidence of the test)?

   b Is it $1 - \beta = P[x > \tau|H_1]$ (the power, or recall, of the test)?

   c Or is it $P[H_1|x > \tau]$ (the precision of the test)?

   d Of the above, what do p-values measure?

   e In finance, the analogous situation is to test whether a variable is involved in a phenomenon. Do p-values tell us anything about the probability that the variable is relevant, given the observed evidence?

2 Consider a medical test where $\alpha = .01$, $\beta = 0$, and the probability of the condition is $P[H_1] = .001$. The test has full recall and a very high confidence. What is the probability that a positive-tested patient is actually sick? Why is it much lower than $1 - \alpha$ and $1 - \beta$? What is the probability that a patient is actually sick after testing positive twice on independent tests?

3 Rerun the examples in Sections 6.3.1 and 6.3.2, where this time you pass an argument sigmaStd=0 to the getTestData function. How do Figures 6.2 and 6.3 look now? What causes the difference, if there is one?

4 Rerun the MDA analysis in Section 6.3.2, where this time you use probability-weighted accuracy (Section 6.4) as the scoring function. Are results materially different? Are they more intuitive or easier to explain? Can you think of other ways to represent MDA outputs using probability-weighted accuracy?

5 Rerun the experiment in Section 6.6, where this time the distance metric used to cluster the features is variation of information (Section 3).

7 Portfolio Construction

7.1 Motivation

The allocation of assets requires making decisions under uncertainty. Markowitz (1952) proposed one of the most influential ideas in modern financial history, namely, the representation of the problem of investing as a convex optimization program. Markowitz's Critical Line Algorithm (CLA) estimates an "efficient frontier" of portfolios that maximize the expected return subject to a given level of risk, where portfolio risk is measured in terms of the standard deviation of returns. In practice, mean-variance optimal solutions tend to be concentrated and unstable (De Miguel et al. 2009).

There are three popular approaches to reducing the instability in optimal portfolios. First, some authors attempted to regularize the solution, by injecting additional information regarding the mean or variance in the form of priors (Black and Litterman 1992). Second, other authors suggested reducing the solution's feasibility region by incorporating additional constraints (Clarke et al. 2002). Third, other authors proposed improving the numerical stability of the covariance matrix's inverse (Ledoit and Wolf 2004).

In Section 2, we discussed how to deal with the instability caused by the noise contained in the covariance matrix. As it turns out, the signal contained in the covariance matrix can also be a source of instability, which requires a specialized treatment. In this section, we explain why certain data structures (or types of signal) make mean-variance solutions unstable, and what we can do to address this second source of instability.

7.2 Convex Portfolio Optimization

Consider a portfolio of N holdings, where its returns in excess of the risk-free rate have an expected value μ and an expected covariance V. Markowitz's insight was to formulate the classical asset allocation problem as a quadratic program,

$$\min_{\omega} \frac{1}{2}\omega'V\omega$$

$$\text{s.t.} : \omega'a = 1,$$

where a characterizes the portfolio's constraints. This problem can be expressed in Lagrangian form as

$$L[\omega,\lambda] = \frac{1}{2}\omega'V\omega - \lambda(\omega'a - 1)$$

with first-order conditions

$$\frac{\partial L[\omega, \lambda]}{\partial \omega} = V\omega - \lambda a$$

$$\frac{\partial L[\omega, \lambda]}{\partial \lambda} = \omega' a - 1.$$

Setting the first-order (necessary) conditions to zero, we obtain that $V\omega - \lambda a = 0 \Rightarrow \omega = \lambda V^{-1} a$ and $\omega' a = a' \omega = 1 \Rightarrow \lambda a' V^{-1} a = 1 \Rightarrow \lambda = 1/(a' V^{-1} a)$, thus

$$\omega^* = \frac{V^{-1} a}{a' V^{-1} a}.$$

The second-order (sufficient) condition confirms that this solution is the minimum of the Lagrangian:

$$\begin{vmatrix} \dfrac{\partial L^2[\omega, \lambda]}{\partial \omega^2} & \dfrac{\partial L^2[\omega, \lambda]}{\partial \omega \partial \lambda} \\ \dfrac{\partial L^2[\omega, \lambda]}{\partial \lambda \partial \omega} & \dfrac{\partial L^2[\omega, \lambda]}{\partial \lambda^2} \end{vmatrix} = \begin{vmatrix} V' & -a' \\ a & 0 \end{vmatrix} = a' a \geq 0.$$

Let us now turn our attention to a few formulations of the characteristic vector, a:

1 For $a = 1_N$ and $V = \sigma I_N$, where $\sigma \in \mathbb{R}^+$, 1_N is a vector of ones of size N, and I_N is an identity matrix of size N, then the solution is the equal weights portfolio (known as the "1/N" portfolio, or the "naïve" portfolio), because $\omega^* = 1_N \sigma^{-1} / (N\sigma^{-1}) = 1_N / N$.
2 For $a = 1_N$ and V is a diagonal matrix with unequal entries ($V_{i,j} = 0$, for all $i \neq j$), then the solution is the inverse-variance portfolio, because $\omega^* = \frac{1}{\sum_{n=1}^{N} \frac{1}{V_{n,n}}} \{\frac{1}{V_{n,n}}\}_{n=1,\ldots,N}$.
3 For $a = 1_N$, the solution is the minimum variance portfolio.
4 For $a = \mu$, the solution maximizes the portfolio's Sharpe ratio, $\omega' \mu / \sqrt{\omega' V \omega}$, and the market portfolio is $V^{-1} \mu / (1_N' V^{-1} \mu)$ (Grinold and Kahn 1999).

7.3 The Condition Number

Certain covariance structures can make the mean-variance optimization solution unstable. To understand why, we need to introduce the concept of condition number of a covariance matrix. Consider a correlation matrix between two securities,

$$C = \begin{bmatrix} 1 & \rho \\ \rho & 1 \end{bmatrix},$$

where ρ is the correlation between their returns. Matrix C can be diagonalized as $CW = W\Lambda$ as follows. First, we set the eigenvalue equation $|C - I\lambda| = 0$. Operating,

$$\begin{vmatrix} 1 - \lambda & \rho \\ \rho & 1 - \lambda \end{vmatrix} = 0 \Rightarrow (1 - \lambda)^2 - \rho^2 = 0.$$

This equation has roots in $\lambda = 1 \pm \rho$, hence the diagonal elements of Λ are

$$\Lambda_{1,1} = 1 + \rho$$

$$\Lambda_{2,2} = 1 - \rho.$$

Second, the eigenvector associated with each eigenvalue is given by the solution to the system

$$\begin{bmatrix} 1 - \Lambda_{1,1} & \rho \\ \rho & 1 - \Lambda_{2,2} \end{bmatrix} \begin{bmatrix} W_{1,1} & W_{1,2} \\ W_{2,1} & W_{2,2} \end{bmatrix} = \begin{bmatrix} 0 & 0 \\ 0 & 0 \end{bmatrix}.$$

If C is not already a diagonal matrix, then $\rho \neq 0$, in which case the above system has solutions in

$$\begin{bmatrix} W_{1,1} & W_{1,2} \\ W_{2,1} & W_{2,2} \end{bmatrix} = \begin{bmatrix} \dfrac{1}{\sqrt{2}} & \dfrac{1}{\sqrt{2}} \\ \dfrac{1}{\sqrt{2}} & -\dfrac{1}{\sqrt{2}} \end{bmatrix},$$

and it is easy to verify that

$$W\Lambda W' = \begin{bmatrix} \dfrac{1}{\sqrt{2}} & \dfrac{1}{\sqrt{2}} \\ \dfrac{1}{\sqrt{2}} & -\dfrac{1}{\sqrt{2}} \end{bmatrix} \begin{bmatrix} 1 + \rho & 0 \\ 0 & 1 - \rho \end{bmatrix} \begin{bmatrix} \dfrac{1}{\sqrt{2}} & \dfrac{1}{\sqrt{2}} \\ \dfrac{1}{\sqrt{2}} & -\dfrac{1}{\sqrt{2}} \end{bmatrix}' = \begin{bmatrix} 1 & \rho \\ \rho & 1 \end{bmatrix} = C.$$

The trace of C is $tr(C) = \Lambda_{1,1} + \Lambda_{2,2} = 2$, so ρ sets how big one eigenvalue gets at the expense of the other. The determinant of C is given by $|C| = \Lambda_{1,1}\Lambda_{2,2} = (1 + \rho)(1 - \rho) = 1 - \rho^2$. The determinant reaches its maximum at $\Lambda_{1,1} = \Lambda_{2,2} = 1$, which corresponds to the uncorrelated case, $\rho = 0$. The determinant reaches its minimum at $\Lambda_{1,1} = 0$ or $\Lambda_{2,2} = 0$, which corresponds to the perfectly correlated case, $|\rho| = 1$. The inverse of C is

$$C^{-1} = W\Lambda^{-1}W' = \frac{1}{|C|}\begin{bmatrix} 1 & -\rho \\ -\rho & 1 \end{bmatrix}.$$

The implication is that the more ρ deviates from zero, the bigger one eigenvalue becomes relative to the other, causing $|C|$ to approach zero, which makes the values of C^{-1} explode.

More generally, the instability caused by covariance structure can be measured in terms of the magnitude between the two extreme eigenvalues. Accordingly, the condition number of a covariance or correlation (or normal, thus diagonalizable) matrix is defined as the absolute value of the ratio between its maximal and minimal (by moduli) eigenvalues. In the above example,

$$\lim_{\rho \to 1^-} \frac{\Lambda_{1,1}}{\Lambda_{2,2}} = +\infty$$

$$\lim_{\rho \to -1^+} \frac{\Lambda_{2,2}}{\Lambda_{1,1}} = +\infty.$$

7.4 Markowitz's Curse

Matrix C is just a standardized version of V, and the conclusions we drew on C^{-1} apply to the V^{-1} used to compute ω^*. When securities within a portfolio are highly correlated ($-1 < \rho \ll 0$ or $0 \ll \rho < 1$), C has a high condition number, and the values of V^{-1} explode. This is problematic in the context of portfolio optimization, because ω^* depends on V^{-1}, and unless $\rho \approx 0$, we must expect an unstable solution to the convex optimization program. In other words, Markowitz's solution is guaranteed to be numerically stable only if $\rho \approx 0$, which is precisely the case when we don't need it! The reason we needed Markowitz was to handle the $\rho \not\approx 0$ case, but the more we need Markowitz, the more numerically unstable is the estimation of ω^*. This is Markowitz's curse.

López de Prado (2016) introduced an ML-based asset allocation method called hierarchical risk parity (HRP). HRP outperforms Markowitz and the naïve allocation in out-of-sample Monte Carlo experiments. The purpose of HRP was not to deliver an optimal allocation, but merely to demonstrate the potential of ML approaches. In fact, HRP outperforms Markowitz out-of-sample even though HRP is by construction suboptimal in-sample. In the next section we analyze further why standard mean-variance optimization is relatively easy to beat.

7.5 Signal as a Source of Covariance Instability

In Section 2, we saw that the covariance instability associated with noise is regulated by the N/T ratio, because the lower bound of the Marcenko–Pastur distribution, λ_-, gets smaller as N/T grows,[22] while the upper bound, λ_+, increases as N/T grows. In this section, we are dealing with a different source of covariance instability, caused by the structure of the data (signal). As we saw in the 2 × 2 matrix example, ρ regulates the matrix's condition number, regardless and independently from N/T. Signal-induced instability is structural, and cannot be reduced by sampling more observations.

There is an intuitive explanation for how signal makes mean-variance optimization unstable. When the correlation matrix is an identity matrix, the eigenvalue function is a horizontal line, and the condition number is 1. Outside that ideal case, the condition number is impacted by irregular correlation structures. In the particular case of finance, when a subset of securities exhibits greater correlation among themselves than to the rest of the investment universe, that subset forms a cluster within the correlation matrix. Clusters appear naturally, as a consequence of hierarchical relationships. When K securities form a cluster, they are more heavily exposed to a common eigenvector, which implies that the associated eigenvalue explains a greater amount of variance. But because the trace of the correlation matrix is exactly N, that means that an eigenvalue can only increase at the expense of the other $K - 1$ eigenvalues in that cluster, resulting in a condition number greater than 1. Consequently, the greater the intracluster correlation is, the higher the condition number becomes. This source of instability is distinct and unrelated to $N/T \rightarrow 1$.

Let us illustrate this intuition with a numerical example. Code Snippet 7.1 shows how to form a block-diagonal correlation matrix of different numbers of blocks, block sizes, and intrablock correlations. Figure 7.1 plots a block-diagonal

SNIPPET 7.1 COMPOSITION OF BLOCK-DIAGONAL CORRELATION MATRICES

```
import matplotlib.pyplot as mpl,seaborn as sns
import numpy as np
#------------------------------------------------------------
corr0=formBlockMatrix(2,2,.5)
eVal,eVec=np.linalg.eigh(corr0)
print max(eVal)/min(eVal)
sns.heatmap(corr0,cmap='viridis')
```

---

[22] As a reminder, in Section 2, variable N denoted the number of columns in the covariance matrix, and variable T denoted the number of independent observations used to compute the covariance matrix.

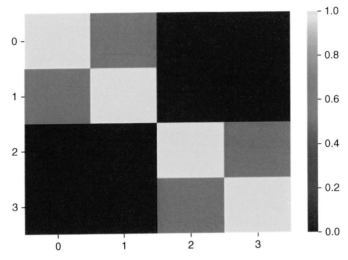

Figure 7.1 Heatmap of a block-diagonal correlation matrix.

matrix of size 4x4, composed of two equal-sized blocks, where the intrablock correlation is 0.5 and the outer-block correlation is zero. Because of this block structure, the condition number is not 1, but 3. The condition number rises if (1) we make one block greater or (2) we increase the intrablock correlation. The reason is, in both cases one eigenvector explains more variance than the rest. For instance, if we increase the size of one block to three and reduce the size of the other to 1, the condition number becomes 4. If instead we increase the intrablock correlation to 0.75, the condition number becomes 7. A block-diagonal correlation matrix of size 500x500 with two equal-sized blocks, where the intrablock correlation is 0.5 has a condition number of 251, again as a result of having 500 eigenvectors where most of the variance is explained by only 2.

Code Snippet 7.2 demonstrates that bringing down the intrablock correlation in only one of the two blocks does not reduce the condition number. The reason is, the extreme eigenvalues are caused by the dominant block. So even though the high condition number may be caused by only one cluster, it impacts the entire correlation matrix. This observation has an important implication: the instability of Markowitz's solution can be traced back to a few dominant

SNIPPET 7.2 BLOCK-DIAGONAL CORRELATION MATRIX WITH A DOMINANT BLOCK

```
corr0=block_diag(formBlockMatrix(1,2,.5))
corr1=formBlockMatrix(1,2,.0)
corr0=block_diag(corr0,corr1)
eVal,eVec=np.linalg.eigh(corr0)
print max(eVal)/min(eVal)
```

clusters within the correlation matrix. We can contain that instability by optimizing the dominant clusters separately, hence preventing that the instability spreads throughout the entire portfolio.

7.6 The Nested Clustered Optimization Algorithm

The remainder of this section is dedicated to introducing a new ML-based method, named nested clustered optimization (NCO), which tackles the source of Markowitz's curse. NCO belongs to a class of algorithms known as "wrappers": it is agnostic as to what member of the efficient frontier is computed, or what set of constraints is imposed. NCO provides a strategy for addressing the effect of Markowitz's curse on an existing mean-variance allocation method.

7.6.1 Correlation Clustering

The first step of the NCO algorithm is to cluster the correlation matrix. This operation involves finding the optimal number of clusters. One possibility is to apply the ONC algorithm (Section 4), however NCO is agnostic as to what particular algorithm is used for determining the number of clusters. For large matrices, where T/N is relatively low, it is advisable to denoise the correlation matrix prior to clustering, following the method described in Section 2. Code Snippet 7.3 implements this procedure. We compute the denoised covariance matrix, cov1, using the deNoiseCov function introduced in Section 2. As a reminder, argument q informs the ratio between the number of rows and the number of columns in the observation matrix. When bWidth=0, the covariance matrix is not denoised. We standardize the resulting covariance matrix into a correlation matrix using the cov2corr function. Then we cluster the cleaned correlation matrix using the clusterKMeansBase function, which we introduced in Section 4. The argument maxNumClusters is set to half the number of columns in the correlation matrix. The reason is, single-item clusters do not cause an increase in the matrix's condition number, so we

---

SNIPPET 7.3 THE CORRELATION CLUSTERING STEP

```
import pandas as pd
cols=cov0.columns
cov1=deNoiseCov(cov0,q,bWidth=.01) # de-noise cov
cov1=pd.DataFrame(cov1,index=cols,columns=cols)
corr1=cov2corr(cov1)
corr1,clstrs,silh=clusterKMeansBase(corr1,
  maxNumClusters=corr0.shape[0]/2,n_init=10)
```

only need to consider clusters with a minimum size of two. If we expect fewer clusters, a lower maxNumClusters may be used to accelerate calculations.

A common question is whether we should cluster corr1 or corr1.abs(). When all correlations are nonnegative, clustering corr1 and corr1.abs() yields the same outcome. When some correlations are negative, the answer is more convoluted, and depends on the numerical properties of the observed inputs. I recommend that you try both, and see what clustering works better for your particular corr1 in Monte Carlo experiments.[23]

7.6.2 Intracluster Weights

The second step of the NCO algorithm is to compute optimal intracluster allocations, using the denoised covariance matrix, cov1. Code Snippet 7.4 implements this procedure. For simplicity purposes, we have defaulted to a minimum variance allocation, as implemented in the minVarPort function. However, nothing in the procedure prevents the use of alternative allocation methods. Using the estimated intracluster weights, we can derive the reduced covariance matrix, cov2, which reports the correlations between clusters.

SNIPPET 7.4 INTRACLUSTER OPTIMAL ALLOCATIONS

```
wIntra=pd.DataFrame(0,index=cov1.index,columns=clstrs.keys())
for i in clstrs:
    wIntra.loc[clstrs[i],i]=minVarPort(cov1.loc[clstrs[i],
        clstrs[i]]).flatten()
cov2=wIntra.T.dot(np.dot(cov1,wIntra)) # reduced covariance matrix
```

7.6.3 Intercluster Weights

The third step of the NCO algorithm is to compute optimal intercluster allocations, using the reduced covariance matrix, cov2. By construction, this covariance matrix is close to a diagonal matrix, and the optimization problem is close to the ideal Markowitz case. In other words, the clustering and intracluster optimization steps have allowed us to transform a "Markowitz-cursed" problem ($|\rho| \gg 0$) into a well-behaved problem ($\rho \approx 0$).

---

[23] As a rule of thumb, corr1.abs() tends to work better in long-short portfolio optimization problems where some correlations are negative. Intuitively, the ability to have negative weights is equivalent to flipping the sign of the correlation, which can induce considerable instability. Because negatively correlated variables will interact through the weights, it makes sense to cluster those variables together, thus containing that source of instability within each cluster.

Code Snippet 7.5 implements this procedure. It applies the same allocation procedure that was used in the intracluster allocation step (that is, in the case of Code Snippet 7.4, the minVarPort function). The final allocation per security is reported by the wAll0 data frame, which results from multiplying intracluster weights with the intercluster weights.

SNIPPET 7.5 INTERCLUSTER OPTIMAL ALLOCATIONS

```
wInter=pd.Series(minVarPort(cov2).flatten(),index=cov2.index)
wAll0=wIntra.mul(wInter,axis=1).sum(axis=1).sort_index()
```

7.7 Experimental Results

In this section we subject the NCO algorithm to controlled experiments, and compare its performance to Markowitz's approach. Like in Section 2, we discuss two characteristic portfolios of the efficient frontier, namely, the minimum variance and maximum Sharpe ratio solutions, since any member of the unconstrained efficient frontier can be derived as a convex combination of the two (a result sometimes known as the "separation theorem").

Code Snippet 7.6 implements the NCO algorithm introduced earlier in this section. When argument mu is None, function optPort_nco returns the minimum variance portfolio, whereas when mu is not None, function optPort_nco returns the maximum Sharpe ratio portfolio.

SNIPPET 7.6 FUNCTION IMPLEMENTING THE NCO ALGORITHM

```
def optPort_nco(cov,mu=None,maxNumClusters=None):
  cov=pd.DataFrame(cov)
  if mu is not None:mu=pd.Series(mu[:,0])
  corr1=cov2corr(cov)
  corr1,clstrs,_=clusterKMeansBase(corr1,maxNumClusters,
    n_init=10)
  wIntra=pd.DataFrame(0,index=cov.index,columns=clstrs.keys())
  for i in clstrs:
    cov_=cov.loc[clstrs[i],clstrs[i]].values
    if mu is None:mu_=None
    else:mu_=mu.loc[clstrs[i]].values.reshape(-1,1)
    wIntra.loc[clstrs[i],i]=optPort(cov_,mu_).flatten()
  cov_=wIntra.T.dot(np.dot(cov,wIntra)) # reduce covariance matrix
  mu_=(None if mu is None else wIntra.T.dot(mu))
  wInter=pd.Series(optPort(cov_,mu_).flatten(),index=cov_.index)
  nco=wIntra.mul(wInter,axis=1).sum(axis=1).values.reshape(-1,1)
  return nco
```

7.7.1 Minimum Variance Portfolio

Code Snippet 7.7 creates a random vector of means and a random covariance matrix that represent a stylized version of a fifty securities portfolio, grouped in ten blocks with intracluster correlations of 0.5. This vector and matrix characterize the "true" process that generates observations.[24] We set a seed for the purpose of reproducing and comparing results across runs with different parameters. Function formTrueMatrix was declared in Section 2.

SNIPPET 7.7 DATA-GENERATING PROCESS

```
nBlocks,bSize,bCorr =10,50,.5
np.random.seed(0)
mu0,cov0=formTrueMatrix(nBlocks,bSize,bCorr)
```

Code Snippet 7.8 uses function simCovMu to simulate a random empirical vector of means and a random empirical covariance matrix based on 1,000 observations drawn from the true process (declared in Section 2). When shrink=True, the empirical covariance matrix is subjected to Ledoit–Wolf shrinkage. Using that empirical covariance matrix, function optPort (also declared in Section 2) estimates the minimum variance portfolio according to Markowitz, and function optPort_nco estimates the minimum variance portfolio applying the NCO algorithm. This procedure is repeated on 1,000 different random empirical covariance matrices. Note that, because minVarPortf=True, the random empirical vectors of means are discarded.

SNIPPET 7.8 DRAWING AN EMPIRICAL VECTOR OF MEANS AND COVARIANCE MATRIX

```
nObs,nSims,shrink,minVarPortf=1000,1000,False,True
np.random.seed(0)
for i in range(nSims):
  mu1,cov1=simCovMu(mu0,cov0,nObs,shrink=shrink)
  if minVarPortf:mu1=None
  w1.loc[i]=optPort(cov1,mu1).flatten()
  w1_d.loc[i]=optPort_nco(cov1,mu1,
    int(cov1.shape[0]/2)).flatten()
```

---

[24] In practical applications, we do not need to simulate $\{\mu, V\}$, as these inputs are estimated from observed data. The reader can repeat this experiment on a pair of observed $\{\mu, V\}$ and evaluate via Monte Carlo the estimation error of alternative optimization methods on those particular inputs, thus finding out what method yields most robust estimates for a particular input.

Code Snippet 7.9 computes the true minimum variance portfolio, derived from the true covariance matrix. Using those allocations as benchmark, it then computes the root-mean-square errors (RMSE) across all weights. We can run Code Snippet 7.9 with and without shrinkage, thus obtaining the four combinations displayed in Figure 7.2.

SNIPPET 7.9 ESTIMATION OF ALLOCATION ERRORS

```
w0=optPort(cov0,None if minVarPortf else mu0)
w0=np.repeat(w0.T,w1.shape[0],axis=0) # true allocation
rmsd=np.mean((w1-w0).values.flatten()**2)**.5 # RMSE
rmsd_d=np.mean((w1_d-w0).values.flatten()**2)**.5 # RMSE
```

	Markowitz	NCO
Raw	7.95E-03	4.21E-03
Shrunk	8.89E-03	6.74E-03

Figure 7.2 RMSE for the minimum variance portfolio.

NCO computes the minimum variance portfolio with 52.98% of Markowitz's RMSE, i.e., a 47.02% reduction in the RMSE. While Ledoit–Wolf shrinkage helps reduce the RMSE, that reduction is relatively small, around 11.81%. Combining shrinkage and NCO yields a 15.30% reduction in RMSE, which is better than shrinkage but worse than NCO alone.

The implication is that NCO delivers substantially lower RMSE than Markowitz's solution, even for a small portfolio of only fifty securities, and that shrinkage adds no value. It is easy to test that NCO's advantage widens for larger portfolios (we leave it as an exercise).

7.7.2 Maximum Sharpe Ratio Portfolio

By setting minVarPortf=False, we can rerun Code Snippets 7.8 and 7.9 to derive the RMSE associated with the maximum Sharpe ratio portfolio. Figure 7.3 reports the results from this experiment.

NCO computes the maximum Sharpe ratio portfolio with 45.17% of Markowitz's RMSE, i.e., a 54.83% reduction in the RMSE. The combination of shrinkage and NCO yields a 18.52% reduction in the RMSE of the maximum Sharpe ratio portfolio, which is better than shrinkage but worse than NCO. Once again, NCO delivers substantially lower RMSE than Markowitz's solution, and shrinkage adds no value.

	Markowitz	NCO
Raw	7.02E-02	3.17E-02
Shrunk	6.54E-02	5.72E-02

Figure 7.3 RMSE for the maximum Sharpe ratio portfolio.

7.8 Conclusions

Markowitz's portfolio optimization framework is mathematically correct, however its practical application suffers from numerical problems. In particular, financial covariance matrices exhibit high condition numbers due to noise and signal. The inverse of those covariance matrices magnifies estimation errors, which leads to unstable solutions: changing a few rows in the observations matrix may produce entirely different allocations. Even if the allocations estimator is unbiased, the variance associated with these unstable solutions inexorably leads to large transaction costs than can erase much of the profitability of these strategies.

In this section, we have traced back the source of Markowitz's instability problems to the shape of the correlation matrix's eigenvalue function. Horizontal eigenvalue functions are ideal for Markowitz's framework. In finance, where clusters of securities exhibit greater correlation among themselves than to the rest of the investment universe, eigenvalue functions are not horizontal, which in turn is the cause for high condition numbers. Signal is the cause of this type of covariance instability, not noise.

We have introduced the NCO algorithm to address this source of instability, by splitting the optimization problem into several problems: computing one optimization per cluster, and computing one final optimization across all clusters. Because each security belongs to one cluster and one cluster only, the final allocation is the product of the intracluster and intercluster weights. Experimental results demonstrate that this dual clustering approach can significantly reduce Markowitz's estimation error. The NCO algorithm is flexible and can be utilized in combination with any other framework, such as Black–Litterman, shrinkage, reversed optimization, or constrained optimization approaches. We can think of NCO as a strategy for splitting the general optimization problem into subproblems, which can then be solved using the researcher's preferred method.

Like many other ML algorithms, NCO is flexible and modular. For example, when the correlation matrix exhibits a strongly hierarchical structure, with clusters within clusters, we can apply the NCO algorithm within each cluster and subcluster, mimicking the matrix's tree-like structure. The goal is to contain the numerical instability at each level of the tree, so that the instability within a subcluster does not extend to its parent cluster or the rest of the correlation matrix.

We can follow the Monte Carlo approach outlined in this section to estimate the allocation error produced by various optimization methods on a particular set of input variables. The result is a precise determination of what method is most robust to a particular case. Thus, rather than relying always on one particular approach, we can apply opportunistically whatever optimization method is best suited in a particular setting.

7.9 Exercises

1 Add to Code Snippet 7.3 a detoning step, and repeat the experimental analysis conducted in Section 7.7. Do you see an additional improvement in NCO's performance? Why?

2 Repeat Section 7.7, where this time you generate covariance matrices without a cluster structure, using the function getRndCov listed in Section 2. Do you reach a qualitatively different conclusion? Why?

3 Repeat Section 7.7, where this time you replace the minVarPort function with the CLA class listed in Bailey and López de Prado (2013).

4 Repeat Section 7.7 for a covariance matrix of size ten and for a covariance matrix of size one hundred. How do NCO's results compare to Markowitz's as a function of the problem's size?

5 Repeat Section 7.7, where you purposely mislead the clusterKMeansBase algorithm by setting its argument maxNumClusters to a very small value, like 2. By how much does NCO's solution worsen? How is it possible that, even with only two clusters (instead of ten), NCO performs significantly better than Markowitz's solution?

8 Testing Set Overfitting

8.1 Motivation

Throughout this Element, we have studied the properties of ML solutions through Monte Carlo experiments. Monte Carlo simulations play in mathematics the analogue to a controlled experiment in the physical sciences. They allow us to reach conclusions regarding the mathematical properties of various estimators and procedures under controlled conditions. Having the ability to control for the conditions of an experiment is essential to being able to make causal inference statements.

A backtest is a historical simulation of how an investment strategy would have performed in the past. It is not a controlled experiment, because we cannot change the environmental variables to derive a new historical time series on which to perform an independent backtest. As a result, backtests cannot help us derive the precise cause–effect mechanisms that make a strategy successful.

This general inability to conduct controlled experiments on investment strategies is more than a technical inconvenience. In the context of strategy development, all we have is a few (relatively short, serially correlated, multicollinear and possibly nonstationary) historical time series. It is easy for a researcher to overfit a backtest, by conducting multiple historical simulations, and selecting the best performing strategy (Bailey et al. 2014). When a researcher presents an overfit backtest as the outcome of a single trial, the simulated performance is inflated. This form of statistical inflation is called selection bias under multiple testing (SBuMT). SBuMT leads to false discoveries: strategies that are replicable in backtests, but fail when implemented.

To make matters worse, SBuMT is compounded at many asset managers, as a consequence of sequential SBuMT at two levels: (1) each researcher runs millions of simulations, and presents the best (overfit) ones to her boss; (2) the company further selects a few backtests among the (already overfit) backtests submitted by the researchers. We may call this backtest hyperfitting, to differentiate it from backtest overfitting (which occurs at the researcher level).

It may take many decades to collect the future (out-of-sample) information needed to debunk a false discovery that resulted from SBuMT. In this section, we study how researchers can estimate the effect that SBuMT has on their findings.

8.2 Precision and Recall

Consider s investment strategies. Some of these strategies are false discoveries, in the sense that their expected return is not positive. We can decompose these strategies between true (s_T) and false (s_F), where $s = s_T + s_F$. Let θ be the odds ratio of true strategies against false strategies, $\theta = s_T/s_F$. In a field like financial economics, where the signal-to-noise ratio is low, false strategies abound, hence θ is expected to be low. The number of true investment strategies is

$$s_T = s\frac{s_T}{s_T + s_F} = s\frac{\frac{s_T}{s_F}}{\frac{s_T + s_F}{s_F}} = s\frac{\theta}{1 + \theta}.$$

Likewise, the number of false investment strategies is

$$s_F = s - s_T = s\left(1 - \frac{\theta}{1 + \theta}\right) = s\frac{1}{1 + \theta}.$$

Given a false positive rate α (type I error), we will obtain a number of false positives, $FP = \alpha s_F$, and a number of true negatives, $TN = (1 - \alpha)s_F$. Let us denote as β the false negative rate (type II error) associated with that α. We will obtain a number of false negatives, $FN = \beta s_T$, and a number of true positives, $TP = (1 - \beta)s_T$. Therefore, the precision and recall of our test are

$$\text{precision} = \frac{TP}{TP + FP} = \frac{(1 - \beta)s_T}{(1 - \beta)s_T + \alpha s_F}$$

$$= \frac{(1 - \beta)s\frac{\theta}{1+\theta}}{(1 - \beta)s\frac{\theta}{1+\theta} + \alpha s\frac{1}{1+\theta}} = \frac{(1 - \beta)\theta}{(1 - \beta)\theta + \alpha}$$

$$\text{recall} = \frac{TP}{TP + FN} = \frac{(1 - \beta)s_T}{(1 - \beta)s_T + \beta s_T} = 1 - \beta.$$

Before running backtests on a strategy, researchers should gather evidence that a strategy may indeed exist. The reason is, the precision of the test is a function of the odds ratio, θ. If the odds ratio is low, the precision will be low, even if we get a positive with high confidence (low p-value).[25] In particular, a strategy is more likely false than true if $(1 - \beta)\theta < \alpha$.

For example, suppose that the probability of a backtested strategy being profitable is 0.01, that is, that one out of one hundred strategies is true, hence $\theta = 1/99$. Then, at the standard thresholds of $\alpha = 0.05$ and $\beta = 0.2$, researchers are expected to get approximately fifty-eight positives out one thousand trials, where approximately eight are true positives, and approximately fifty are false positives. Under these circumstances, a p-value of 0.05 implies a false discovery rate of 86.09% (roughly 50/58). For this reason alone, we should expect that most discoveries in financial econometrics are likely false.

---

[25] This argument leads to the same conclusion we reached in Section 6: p-values report a rather uninformative probability. It is possible for a statistical test to have high confidence (low p-value) and low precision.

8.3 Precision and Recall under Multiple Testing

After one trial, the probability of making a type I error is α. Suppose that we repeat for a second time a test with false positive probability α. At each trial, the probability of *not* making a type I error is $(1 - \alpha)$. If the two trials are independent, the probability of not making a type I error on the first *and* second tests is $(1 - \alpha)^2$. The probability of making *at least one* type I error is the complement, $1 - (1 - \alpha)^2$. If we conduct K independent trials, the joint probability of not making a single type I error is $(1 - \alpha)^K$. Hence, the probability of making at least one type I error is the complement, $\alpha_K = 1 - (1 - \alpha)^K$. This is also known as the familywise error rate (FWER).

After one trial, the probability of making a type II error is β. After K independent trials, the probability of making a type II error on all of them is $\beta_K = \beta^K$. Note the difference with FWER. In the false positive case, we are interested in the probability of making *at least one* error. This is because a single false alarm is a failure. However, in the false negative case, we are interested in the probability that *all* positives are missed. As K increases, α_K grows and β_K shrinks.

The precision and recall adjusted for multiple testing are

$$\text{precision} = \frac{(1 - \beta_K)\theta}{(1 - \beta_K)\theta + \alpha_K} = \frac{(1 - \beta^K)\theta}{(1 - \beta^K)\theta + 1 - (1 - \alpha)^K}$$

$$\text{recall} = 1 - \beta_K = 1 - \beta^K.$$

8.4 The Sharpe Ratio

Financial analysts do not typically assess the performance of a strategy in terms of precision and recall. The most common measure of strategy performance is the Sharpe ratio. In what follows, we will develop a framework for assessing the probability that a strategy is false. The inputs are the Sharpe ratio estimate, as well as metadata captured during the discovery process.[26]

Consider an investment strategy with excess returns (or risk premia) $\{r_t\}$, $t = 1, \ldots, T$, which are independent and identically distributed (IID) Normal,

$$r_t \sim \mathcal{N}[\mu, \sigma^2],$$

---

[26] Perhaps analysts should use precision and recall instead of the Sharpe ratio, but that's beyond the point. Financial mathematicians rarely have the luxury of framing the problems they work on, unlike topologists, set theorists, algebraic geometers, etc.

where $\mathcal{N}[\mu, \sigma^2]$ represents a Normal distribution with mean μ and variance σ^2. Following Sharpe (1966, 1975, 1994), the (nonannualized) Sharpe Ratio of such strategy is defined as

$$SR = \frac{\mu}{\sigma}.$$

Because parameters μ and σ are not known, SR is estimated as

$$\widehat{SR} = \frac{E[\{r_t\}]}{\sqrt{V[\{r_t\}]}}.$$

Under the assumption that returns are IID Normal, Lo (2002) derived the asymptotic distribution of $\widehat{SR}$ as

$$\left(\widehat{SR} - SR\right) \xrightarrow{a} \mathcal{N}\left[0, \frac{1 + \frac{1}{2}SR^2}{T}\right].$$

However, empirical evidence shows that hedge fund returns exhibit substantial negative skewness and positive excess kurtosis (among others, see Brooks and Kat 2002; Ingersoll et al. 2007). Wrongly assuming that returns are IID Normal can lead to a gross underestimation of the false positive probability.

Under the assumption that returns are drawn from IID non-Normal distributions, Mertens (2002) derived the asymptotic distribution of $\widehat{SR}$ as

$$\left(\widehat{SR} - SR\right) \xrightarrow{a} \mathcal{N}\left[0, \frac{1 + \frac{1}{2}SR^2 - \gamma_3 SR + \frac{\gamma_4 - 3}{4}SR^2}{T}\right],$$

where γ_3 is the skewness of $\{r_t\}$, and γ_4 is the kurtosis of $\{r_t\}$ ($\gamma_3 = 0$ and $\gamma_4 = 3$ when returns follow a Normal distribution). Shortly after, Christie (2005) and Opdyke (2007) discovered that, in fact, Mertens's equation is also valid under the more general assumption that returns are stationary and ergodic (not necessarily IID). The key implication is that $\hat{SR}$ still follows a Normal distribution even if returns are non-Normal, however with a variance that partly depends on the skewness and kurtosis of the returns.

8.5 The "False Strategy" Theorem

A researcher may carry out a large number of historical simulations (trials), and report only the best outcome (maximum Sharpe ratio). The distribution of the maximum Sharpe ratio is not the same as the distribution of a Sharpe ratio randomly chosen among the trials, hence giving rise to SBuMT. When more than one trial takes place, the expected value of the maximum Sharpe ratio is greater than the expected value of the Sharpe ratio from a random trial. In particular, given an investment strategy with expected Sharpe ratio zero and nonnull variance, the expected value of the maximum Sharpe ratio is strictly positive, and a function of the number of trials.

Given the above, the magnitude of SBuMT can be expressed in terms of the difference between the expected maximum Sharpe ratio and the expected Sharpe ratio from a random trial (zero, in the case of a false strategy). As it turns out, SBuMT is a function of two variables: the number of trials, and the variance of the Sharpe ratios across trials. The following theorem formally states that relationship. A proof can be found in Appendix B.

Theorem: Given a sample of estimated performance statistics $\{\widehat{SR}_k\}$, $k = 1, \ldots, K$, drawn from independent and identically distributed Gaussians, $\widehat{SR}_k \sim \mathcal{N}[0, V[\widehat{SR}_k]]$, then

$$E\left[\max_k\{\widehat{SR}_k\}\right]\left(V\left[\{\widehat{SR}_k\}\right]\right)^{-\frac{1}{2}} \approx (1 - \gamma)Z^{-1}\left[1 - \frac{1}{K}\right] + \gamma Z^{-1}\left[1 - \frac{1}{Ke}\right],$$

where $Z^{-1}[.]$ is the inverse of the standard Gaussian CDF, $E[.]$ is the expected value, $V[.]$ is the variance, e is Euler's number, and γ is the Euler–Mascheroni constant.

8.6 Experimental Results

The False Strategy theorem provides us with an approximation of the expected maximum Sharpe ratio. An experimental analysis of this theorem can be useful at two levels. First, it can help us find evidence that the theorem is not true, and in fact the proof is flawed. Of course, the converse is not true: experimental evidence can never replace the role of a mathematical proof. Still, experimental evidence can point to problems with the proof, and give us a better understanding of what the proof should look like. Second, the theorem does not provide a boundary for the approximation. An experimental analysis can help us estimate the distribution of the approximation error.

The following Monte Carlo experiment evaluates the accuracy of the False Strategy theorem. First, given a pair of values $(K, V[\{\widehat{SR}_k\}])$, we generate a random array of size (SxK), where S is the number of Monte Carlo experiments. The values contained by this random array are drawn from a Standard Normal distribution. Second, the rows in this array are centered and scaled to match zero mean and $V[\{\widehat{SR}_k\}]$ variance. Third, the maximum value across each row is computed, $\max_k\{\widehat{SR}_k\}$, resulting in a number S of such maxima. Fourth, we compute the average value across the S maxima, $\hat{E}[\max_k\{\widehat{SR}_k\}]$. Fifth, this empirical (Monte Carlo) estimate of the expected maximum SR can then be compared with the analytical solution provided by the False Strategy theorem, $E[\max_k\{\widehat{SR}_k\}]$. Sixth, the estimation error is defined in relative terms to the predicted value, as

$$\varepsilon = \frac{\hat{E}[\max_k\{\widehat{SR}_k\}]}{E[\max_k\{\widehat{SR}_k\}]} - 1.$$

Seventh, we repeat the previous steps R times, resulting in $\{\varepsilon_r\}_{r=1,\dots,R}$ estimation errors, allowing us to compute the mean and standard deviation of the estimation errors associated with K trials. Code Snippet 8.1 implements this Monte Carlo experiment in python.

SNIPPET 8.1 EXPERIMENTAL VALIDATION OF THE FALSE STRATEGY THEOREM

```
import numpy as np,pandas as pd
from scipy.stats import norm,percentileofscore
#- - - - - - - - - - - - - - - - - - - - - - - - - - - - - - - - - - - - - 
def getExpectedMaxSR(nTrials,meanSR,stdSR):
    # Expected max SR, controlling for SBuMT
    emc=0.5772156649015328606065120900824024310421591336
    sr0=(1-emc)*norm.ppf(1-1./nTrials)+/
        emc*norm.ppf(1-(nTrials*np.e)**-1)
    sr0=meanSR+stdSR*sr0
    return sr0
#- - - - - - - - - - - - - - - - - - - - - - - - - - - - - - - - - - - - - 
def getDistMaxSR(nSims,nTrials,stdSR,meanSR):
    # Monte Carlo of max{SR} on nTrials, from nSims simulations
    rng=np.random.RandomState()
    out=pd.DataFrame()
    for nTrials_ in nTrials:
        #1) Simulated Sharpe ratios
        sr=pd.DataFrame(rng.randn(nSims,nTrials_))
        sr=sr.sub(sr.mean(axis=1),axis=0) # center
        sr=sr.div(sr.std(axis=1),axis=0) # scale
        sr=meanSR+sr*stdSR
        #2) Store output
        out_=sr.max(axis=1).to_frame('max{SR}')
        out_['nTrials']=nTrials_
        out=out.append(out_,ignore_index=True)
    return out
#- - - - - - - - - - - - - - - - - - - - - - - - - - - - - - - - - - - - - 
```

```
if __name__=='__main__':
  nTrials=list(set(np.logspace(1,6,1000).astype(int)));nTrials.sort()
  sr0=pd.Series({i:getExpectedMaxSR(i,meanSR=0,stdSR=1) \
    for i in nTrials})
  sr1=getDistMaxSR(nSims=1E3,nTrials=nTrials,meanSR=0,
    stdSR=1)
```

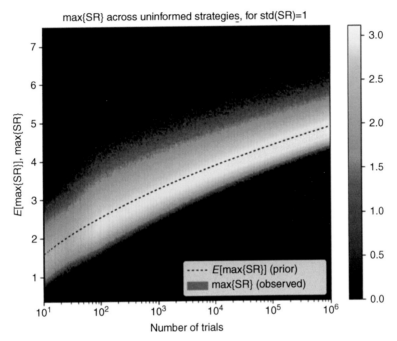

Figure 8.1 Comparison of experimental and theoretical results from the False Strategy theorem.

Figure 8.1 helps us visualize the outcomes from this experiment, for a wide range of trials (in the plot, between 2 and 1 million). For $V[\{\widehat{SR}_k\}] = 1$ and any given number of trials K, we simulate the maximum Sharpe ratio 10,000 times, so that we can derive the distribution of maximum Sharpe ratios. The y-axis shows that distribution of the maximum Sharpe ratios ($\max_k\{\widehat{SR}_k\}$) for each number of trials K (x-axis), when the true Sharpe ratio is zero. Results with a higher probability receive a lighter color. For instance, if we conduct 1,000 trials, the expected maximum Sharpe ratio (E[$\max_k\{\widehat{SR}_k\}$]) is 3.26, even though the true Sharpe ratio of the strategy is null. As expected, there is a raising hurdle that the researcher must beat as he conducts more backtests. We can compare these experimental results with the results predicted by the False Strategy theorem, which are represented with a dashed line. The comparison of these two results (experiments and theoretical) seems to indicate that the False Strategy theorem accurately estimates the expected maximum SR for the range of trials studied.

We turn now our attention to evaluating the precision of the theorem's approximation. We define the approximation error as the difference between the experimental prediction (based on 1,000 simulations) and the theorem's prediction, divided by the theorem's prediction. We can then reevaluate these estimation errors one hundred times for each number of trials K and derive the mean and standard deviation of the errors. Code Snippet 8.2 implements a second Monte Carlo experiment that evaluates the accuracy of the theorem.

SNIPPET 8.2 MEAN AND STANDARD DEVIATION OF THE PREDICTION ERRORS

```
def getMeanStdError(nSims0,nSims1,nTrials,stdSR=1,meanSR=0):
    # Compute standard deviation of errors per nTrial
    # nTrials: [number of SR used to derive max{SR}]
    # nSims0: number of max{SR} used to estimate E[max{SR}]
    # nSims1: number of errors on which std is computed
    sr0=pd.Series({i:getExpectedMaxSR(i,meanSR,stdSR) \
        for i in nTrials})
    sr0=sr0.to_frame('E[max{SR}]')
    sr0.index.name='nTrials'
    err=pd.DataFrame()
    for i in xrange(int(nSims1)):
        sr1=getDistDSR(nSims=1E3,nTrials=nTrials,meanSR=0,
          stdSR=1)
        sr1=sr1.groupby('nTrials').mean()
        err_=sr0.join(sr1).reset_index()
        err_['err']=err_['max{SR}']/err_['E[max{SR}]']-1.
        err=err.append(err_)
    out={'meanErr':err.groupby('nTrials')['err'].mean()}
    out['stdErr']=err.groupby('nTrials')['err'].std()
    out=pd.DataFrame.from_dict(out,orient='columns')
    return out
#- - - - - - - - - - - - - - - - - - - - - - - - - - - - -
if __name__=='__main__':
  nTrials=list(set(np.logspace(1,6,1000).astype(int)));nTrials.sort()
  stats=getMeanStdError(nSims0=1E3,nSims1=1E2,
    nTrials=nTrials,stdSR=1)
```

Figure 8.2 plots the results from this second experiment. The circles represent average errors relative to predicted values (y-axis), computed for alternative numbers of trials (x-axis). From this result, it appears that the False Strategy theorem produces asymptotically unbiased estimates. Only at $K \approx 50$, the theorem's estimate exceeds the experimental value by approx. 0.7%.

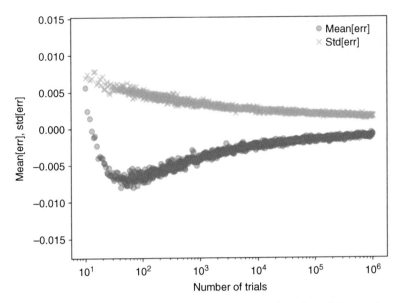

Figure 8.2 Statistics of the approximation errors as a function of the number of trials.

The crosses represent the standard deviation of the errors (y-axis), derived for different numbers of trials (x-axis). From this experiment, we can deduce that the standard deviations are relatively small, below 0.5% of the values forecasted by the theorem, and they become smaller as the number of trials raises.

8.7 The Deflated Sharpe Ratio

The main conclusion from the False Strategy theorem is that, unless $\max_k\{\widehat{SR}_k\} \gg E[\max_k\{\widehat{SR}_k\}]$, the discovered strategy is likely to be a *false positive*. If we can compute $E[\max_k\{\widehat{SR}_k\}]$, we can use that value to set the null hypothesis that must be rejected to conclude that the performance of the strategy is statistically significant, $H_0 = E[\max_k\{\widehat{SR}_k\}]$. Then, the deflated Sharpe ratio (Bailey and López de Prado 2014) can be derived as

$$\widehat{DSR} = Z\left[\frac{\left(\widehat{SR} - E\left[\max_k\{\widehat{SR}_k\}\right]\right)\sqrt{T-1}}{\sqrt{1 - \hat{\gamma}_3\widehat{SR} + \frac{\hat{\gamma}_4-1}{4}\widehat{SR}^2}}\right].$$

$\widehat{DSR}$ can be interpreted as the probability of observing a Sharpe ratio greater or equal to $\widehat{SR}$ subject to the null hypothesis that the true Sharpe ratio is zero, while adjusting for skewness, kurtosis, sample length, and multiple testing. The calculation of $\widehat{DSR}$ requires the estimation of $E[\max_k\{\widehat{SR}_k\}]$, which in turn requires the estimation of K and $V[\{\widehat{SR}_k\}]$. Here is where ML comes to our rescue, as explained next.

8.7.1 Effective Number of Trials

The False Strategy theorem requires knowledge of the number of independent trials within a family of tests. However, it is uncommon for financial researchers to run independent trials. A more typical situation is for researchers to try different strategies, where multiple trials are run for each strategy. Trials associated with one strategy presumably have higher correlations to one another than to other strategies. This relationship pattern can be visualized as a block correlation matrix. For example, Figure 8.3 plots a real example of a correlation matrix between 6,385 backtested returns series for the same investment universe, before and after clustering (for a detailed description of this example, see López de Prado 2019a). The ONC algorithm (Section 4) discovers the existence of four differentiated strategies. Hence, in this example we would estimate that $E[K] = 4$. This is a conservative estimate, since the true number K of independent strategies must be smaller than the number of low-correlated strategies.

8.7.2 Variance across Trials

In this section, we follow closely López de Prado and Lewis (2018). Upon completion of the clustering above, ONC has successfully partitioned our N strategies into K groups, each of which is construed of highly correlated strategies. We can further utilize this clustering to reduce the N strategies to $K \ll N$ cluster-level strategies. Upon creation of these "cluster strategies," we derive our estimate of $V[\{\widehat{SR}_k\}]$, where $k = 1, \dots, K$.

For a given cluster k, the goal is to form an aggregate cluster returns time series $S_{k,t}$. This necessitates choosing a weighting scheme for the aggregation. A good candidate is the minimum variance allocation, because it prevents that individual trials with high variance dominate the cluster's returns. Let C_k denote the set of strategies in cluster k, Σ_k the covariance matrix restricted to strategies in C_k, $r_{i,t}$ the returns series for strategy $i \in C_k$, and $w_{k,i}$ the weight associated with strategy $i \in C_k$. Then, we compute

$$\{w_{k,i}\}_{i \in C_k} = \frac{\Sigma_k^{-1} 1_k}{1_k' \Sigma_k^{-1} 1_k}$$

$$S_{k,t} = \sum_{i \in C_k} w_{k,i} r_{i,t},$$

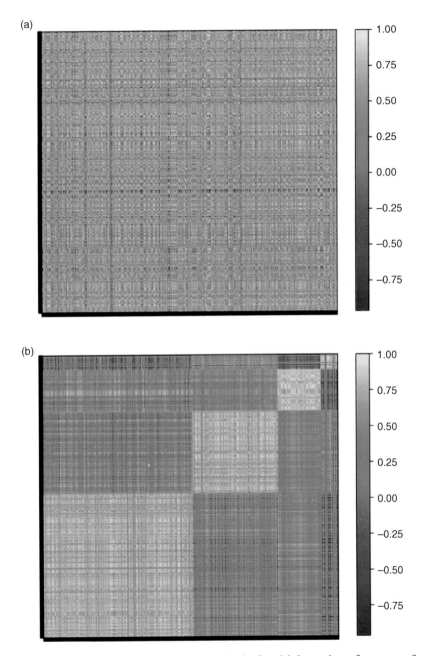

Figure 8.3 Clustering of 6,385 trials, typical of multiple testing of a group of strategies, before and after clustering.

Source: López de Prado (2019a)

where 1_k is the characteristic vector of $1s$, of size $||C_k||$. A robust method of computing w_k can be found in López de Prado and Lewis (2018). With the cluster returns time series $S_{k,t}$ now computed, we estimate each SR ($\widehat{SR}_k$). However, these $\widehat{SR}_k$ are not yet comparable, as their betting frequency may vary. To make them comparable, we must first annualize each. Accordingly, we calculate the average number of bets per year as

$$\text{Years}_k = \frac{\text{Last Date}_k - \text{First Date}_k}{365.25}$$

$$\text{Frequency}_k = \frac{T_k}{\text{Years}_k},$$

where T_k is the length of the $S_{k,t}$, and First Date$_k$ and Last Date$_k$ are the first and last dates of trading for $S_{k,t}$, respectively. With this, we estimate the annualized Sharpe ratio (aSR) as

$$\widehat{\text{aSR}}_k = \frac{E[\{S_{k,t}\}]\text{Frequency}_k}{\sqrt{V[\{S_{k,t}\}]\text{Frequency}_k}} = \widehat{\text{SR}}_k \sqrt{\text{Frequency}_k}.$$

With these now comparable $\widehat{\text{aSR}}_k$, we can estimate the variance of clustered trials as

$$E[V[\{\widehat{\text{SR}}_k\}]] = \frac{V[\{\widehat{\text{aSR}}_k\}]}{\text{Frequency}_{k^*}},$$

where Frequency$_{k^*}$ is the frequency of the selected cluster, k^*. The above equation expresses the estimated variance of clustered trials in terms of the frequency of the selected strategy, in order to match the (nonannualized) frequency of the $\widehat{\text{SR}}$ estimate.

8.8 Familywise Error Rate

This section has so far explained how to derive the probability that an investment strategy is false, using the False Strategy theorem. In this section we discuss an alternative method, which relies on the notion of familywise error rate.

Under the standard Neyman–Pearson hypothesis testing framework, we reject a null hypothesis H_0 with confidence $(1 - \alpha)$ when we observe an event that, should the null hypothesis be true, could only occur with probability α. Then, the probability of falsely rejecting the null hypothesis (type I error) is α. This is also known as the probability of a false positive.

When Neyman and Pearson (1933) proposed this framework, they did not consider the possibility of conducting multiple tests and select the best outcome. As we saw in Section 8.3, when a test is repeated multiple times, the combined false positive probability increases. After a "family" of K independent tests, we would reject H_0 with confidence $(1 - \alpha)^K$, hence the "family" false positive probability (or familywise error rate, FWER) is $\alpha_K = 1 - (1 - \alpha)^K$. This is the probability that *at least one* of the positives is false, which is the complement to the probability that none of the positives is false, $(1 - \alpha)^K$.

8.8.1 Šidàk's Correction

Suppose that we set a FWER over K independent tests at α_K. Then, the individual false positive probability can be derived from the above equation as $\alpha = 1 - (1 - \alpha_K)^{1/K}$. This is known as the Šidàk correction for multiple testing (Šidàk 1967), and it can be approximated as the first term of a Taylor expansion, $\alpha \approx \alpha_K / K$ (known as Bonferroni's approximation).

As we did earlier, we can apply the ONC algorithm to estimate E[K]. While it is true that the E[K] trials are not perfectly uncorrelated, they provide a conservative estimate of the minimum number of clusters the algorithm could not reduce further. With this estimate E[K], we can apply Šidàk's correction, and compute the type I error probability under multiple testing, α_K.

8.8.2 Type I Errors under Multiple Testing

Consider an investment strategy with returns time series of size T. We estimate the Sharpe ratio, $\widehat{SR}$, and subject that estimate to a hypothesis test, where $H_0 : SR = 0$ and $H_1 : SR > 0$. We wish to determine the probability of a false positive when this test is applied multiple times.

Bailey and López de Prado (2012) derived the probability that the true Sharpe ratio exceeds a given threshold SR^*, under the general assumption that returns are stationary and ergodic (not necessarily IID Normal). If the true Sharpe ratio equals SR^*, the statistic $\hat{z}[SR^*]$ is asymptotically distributed as a Standard Normal,

$$\hat{z}[SR^*] = \frac{\left(\widehat{SR} - SR^*\right)\sqrt{T - 1}}{\sqrt{1 - \hat{\gamma}_3 \widehat{SR} + \frac{\hat{\gamma}_4 - 1}{4} \widehat{SR}^2}} \xrightarrow{a} Z,$$

where $\widehat{SR}$ is the estimated Sharpe ratio (nonannualized), T is the number of observations, $\hat{\gamma}_3$ is the skewness of the returns, and $\hat{\gamma}_4$ is the kurtosis of the returns. Familywise type I errors occur with probability

$$P[\max_k \{\hat{z}[0]_k\}_{k=1,\ldots,K} > z_\alpha | H_0] = 1 - (1-\alpha)^K = \alpha_K.$$

For a FWER α_K, Šidàk's correction gives us a single-trial significance level $\alpha = 1 - (1-\alpha_K)^{1/K}$. Then, the null hypothesis is rejected with confidence $(1-\alpha_K)$ if $\max_k \{\hat{z}[0]_k\}_{k=1,\ldots,K} > z_\alpha$, where z_α is the critical value of the Standard Normal distribution that leaves a probability α to the right, $z_\alpha = Z^{-1}[1-\alpha] = Z^{-1}[(1-\alpha_K)^{1/K}]$, and $Z[.]$ is the CDF of the standard Normal distribution.

Conversely, we can derive the type I error under multiple testing (α_K) as follows: first, apply the clustering procedure on the trials correlation matrix, to estimate clusters' returns series and $E[K]$; second, estimate $\hat{z}[0] = \max_k \{\hat{z}[0]_k\}_{k=1,\ldots,K}$ on the selected cluster's returns; third, compute the type I error for a single test, $\alpha = 1 - Z[\hat{z}[0]]$; fourth, correct for multiple testing, $\alpha_K = 1 - (1-\alpha)^K$, resulting in

$$\alpha_K = 1 - Z[\hat{z}[0]]^{E[K]}.$$

Let us illustrate the above calculations with a numerical example. Suppose that after conducting 1,000 trials, we identify an investment strategy with a Sharpe ratio of 0.0791 (nonannualized), skewness of -3, kurtosis of 10, computed on 1,250 daily observations (five years, at 250 annual observations). These levels of skewness and kurtosis are typical of hedge fund returns sampled with daily frequency. From these inputs we derive $\hat{z}[0] \approx 2.4978$ and $\alpha \approx 0.0062$. At this type I error probability, most researchers would reject the null hypothesis, and declare that a new investment strategy has been found. However, this α is not adjusted for the $E[K]$ trials it took to find this strategy. We apply our ONC algorithm, and conclude that out of the 1,000 (correlated) trials, there are $E[K] = 10$ effectively independent trials (again, with "effectively" independent we do not assert that the ten clusters are strictly independent, but that the algorithm could not find more uncorrelated groupings). Then, the corrected FWER is $\alpha_K \approx 0.0608$. Even though the annualized Sharpe ratio is approx. 1.25, the probability that this strategy is a false discovery is relatively high, for two reasons: (1) the number of trials, since $\alpha_K = \alpha \approx 0.0062$ if $E[K] = 1$; (2) the non-Normality of the returns, since $\alpha_K \approx 0.0261$ should returns have been Normal. As expected, wrongly assuming Normal returns leads to a gross underestimation of the type I error probability. Code Snippet 8.3 provides the python code that replicates these results.

SNIPPET 8.3 TYPE I ERROR, WITH NUMERICAL EXAMPLE

```
import scipy.stats as ss
#-------------------------------------------------------
def getZStat(sr,t,sr_=0,skew=0,kurt=3):
   z=(sr-sr_)*(t-1)**.5
   z/=(1-skew*sr+(kurt-1)/4.*sr**2)**.5
   return z
#-------------------------------------------------------
def type1Err(z,k=1):
  # false positive rate
  alpha=ss.norm.cdf(-z)
  alpha_k=1-(1-alpha)**k # multi-testing correction
  return alpha_k
#-------------------------------------------------------
def main0():
  # Numerical example
  t,skew,kurt,k,freq=1250,-3,10,10,250
  sr=1.25/freq**.5;sr_=1./freq**.5
  z=getZStat(sr,t,0,skew,kurt)
  alpha_k=type1Err(z,k=k)
  print alpha_k
  return
#-------------------------------------------------------
if __name__=='__main__':main0()
```

8.8.3 Type II Errors under Multiple Testing

Suppose that the alternative hypothesis ($H_1 : SR > 0$) for the best strategy is true, and $SR = SR^*$. Then, the power of the test associated with a FWER α_K is

$$P[\max_k \{\hat{z}[0]_k\}_{k=1,\ldots,K} > z_\alpha | SR = SR^*]$$

$$= P\left[\frac{\left(\widehat{SR} + SR^* - SR^*\right)\sqrt{T-1}}{\sqrt{1 - \hat{\gamma}_3 \widehat{SR} + \frac{\hat{\gamma}_4 - 1}{4} \widehat{SR}^2}} > z_\alpha | SR = SR^*\right]$$

$$= P\left[\hat{z}[SR^*] > z_\alpha - \frac{SR^* \sqrt{T-1}}{\sqrt{1 - \hat{\gamma}_3 \widehat{SR} + \frac{\hat{\gamma}_4 - 1}{4} \widehat{SR}^2}} | SR = SR^*\right]$$

$$= 1 - P\left[\hat{z}[SR^*] < z_\alpha - \frac{SR^* \sqrt{T-1}}{\sqrt{1 - \hat{\gamma}_3 \widehat{SR} + \frac{\hat{\gamma}_4 - 1}{4} \widehat{SR}^2}} | SR = SR^*\right]$$

$$= 1 - Z \left[z_\alpha - \frac{\mathrm{SR}^* \sqrt{T-1}}{\sqrt{1 - \hat{\gamma}_3 \widehat{\mathrm{SR}} + \frac{\hat{\gamma}_4 - 1}{4} \widehat{\mathrm{SR}}^2}} \right] = 1 - \beta,$$

where $z_\alpha = Z^{-1}[(1 - \alpha_K)^{1/K}]$. Accordingly, the *individual* power of the test increases with SR^*, sample length, and skewness, however it decreases with kurtosis. This probability $(1 - \beta)$ is alternatively known as the true positive rate, power, or recall.

In Section 8.3, we defined the familywise false negative (miss) probability as the probability that *all* individual positives are missed, $\beta_K = \beta^K$. For a given pair (α_K, β_K), we can derive the pair (α, β) and imply the value SR^* such that $P[\max_k \{\hat{z}[0]_k\}_{k=1,\ldots,K} > z_\alpha | SR = SR^*] = 1 - \beta$. The interpretation is that, at a FWER α_K, achieving a familywise power above $(1 - \beta_K)$ requires that the true Sharpe ratio exceeds SR^*. In other words, the test is not powerful enough to detect true strategies with a Sharpe ratio below that implied SR^*.

We can derive the Type II error under multiple testing (β_K) as follows: first, given a FWER α_K, which is either set exogenously or it is estimated as explained in the previous section, compute the single-test critical value, z_α; second, the probability of missing a strategy with Sharpe ratio SR^* is $\beta = Z[z_\alpha - \theta]$, where

$$\theta = \frac{\mathrm{SR}^* \sqrt{T-1}}{\sqrt{1 - \hat{\gamma}_3 \widehat{\mathrm{SR}} + \frac{\hat{\gamma}_4 - 1}{4} \widehat{\mathrm{SR}}^2}};$$

third, from the individual false negative probability, we derive $\beta_K = \beta^K$ as the probability that all positives are missed.

Let us apply the above equations to the numerical example in the previous section. There, we estimated that the FWER was $\alpha_K \approx 0.0608$, which implies a critical value $z_\alpha \approx 2.4978$. Then, the probability of missing a strategy with a true Sharpe ratio $SR^* \approx 0.0632$ (nonannualized) is $\beta \approx 0.6913$, where $\theta \approx 1.9982$. This high individual Type II error probability is understandable, because the test is not powerful enough to detect such a weak signal (an annualized Sharpe ratio of only 1.0) after a single trial. But because we have conducted ten trials, $\beta_K \approx 0.0249$. The test detects more than 97.5% of the strategies with a true Sharpe ratio $SR^* \geq 0.0632$. Code Snippet 8.4 provides the python code that replicates these results (see Code Snippet 8.3 for functions getZStat and type1Err).

SNIPPET 8.4 TYPE II ERROR, WITH NUMERICAL EXAMPLE

```
def getTheta(sr,t,sr_=0,skew=0,kurt=3):
  theta=sr_*(t-1)**.5
  theta/=(1-skew*sr+(kurt-1)/4.*sr**2)**.5
  return theta
#- - - - - - - - - - - - - - - - - - - - - - - - - - - - - - - - - - - - - - - - - - -
def type2Err(alpha_k,k,theta):
  # false negative rate
  z=ss.norm.ppf((1-alpha_k)**(1./k)) # Sidak's correction
  beta=ss.norm.cdf(z-theta)
  return beta
#- - - - - - - - - - - - - - - - - - - - - - - - - - - - - - - - - - - - - - - - - - -
def main0():
  # Numerical example
  t,skew,kurt,k,freq=1250,-3,10,10,250
  sr=1.25/freq**.5;sr_=1./freq**.5
  z=getZStat(sr,t,0,skew,kurt)
  alpha_k=type1Err(z,k=k)
  theta=getTheta(sr,t,sr_,skew,kurt)
  beta=type2Err(alpha_k,k,theta)
  beta_k=beta**k
  print beta_k
  return
#- - - - - - - - - - - - - - - - - - - - - - - - - - - - - - - - - - - - - - - - - - -
if __name__=='__main__':main0()
```

8.8.4 The Interaction between Type I and Type II Errors

Figure 8.4 illustrates the interrelation between α and β. The top distribution models the probability of $\widehat{SR}$ estimates under the assumption that H_0 is true. The bottom distribution (plotted upside down, to facilitate display) models the probability of $\widehat{SR}$ estimates under the assumption that H_1 is true, and in particular under the scenario where $SR^* = 1$. The sample length, skewness, and kurtosis influence the variance of these two distributions. Given an actual estimate $\widehat{SR}$, those variables determine the probabilities α and β, where decreasing one implies increasing the other. In most journal articles, authors focus on the "top" distribution and ignore the "bottom" distribution.

The analytic solution we derived for Type II errors makes it obvious that this trade-off also exists between α_K and β_K, although in a not so straightforward manner as in the $K = 1$ case. Figure 8.5 shows that, for a fixed α_K, as K increases, α decreases, z_α increases, hence β increases.

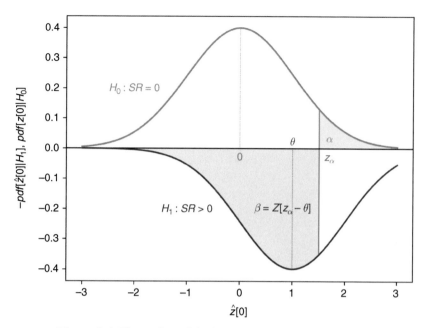

Figure 8.4 Illustration of the interrelation between α and β.

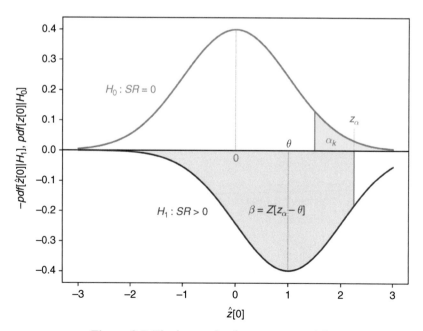

Figure 8.5 The interaction between α_K and β.

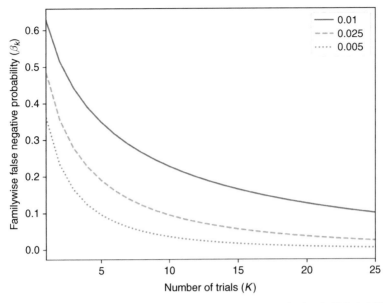

Figure 8.6 β_K as K increases for $\theta \approx 1.9982$ and $\alpha_K \in \{0.01, 0.025, 0.05\}$.

Figure 8.6 plots β_K as K increases for various levels of α_K. Although β increases with K, the overall effect is to decrease β_K. For a fixed α_K, the equation that determines β_K as a function of K and θ is

$$\beta_K = \left(Z[Z^{-1}[(1 - \alpha_K)^{1/K}] - \theta]\right)^K.$$

8.9 Conclusions

The Sharpe ratio of an investment strategy under a single trial follows a Gaussian distribution, even if the strategy returns are non-Normal (still, returns must be stationary and ergodic). Researchers typically conduct a multiplicity of trials, and selecting out of them the best performing strategy increases the probability of selecting a false strategy. In this section, we have studied two alternative procedures to evaluate the extent to which testing set overfitting invalidates a discovered investment strategy.

The first approach relies on the False Strategy theorem. This theorem derives the expected value of the maximum Sharpe ratio, $\mathrm{E}[\max_k\{\widehat{\mathrm{SR}}_k\}]$, as a function of the number of trials, K, and the variance of the Sharpe ratios across the trials, $\mathrm{V}[\{\widehat{\mathrm{SR}}_k\}]$. ML methods allow us to estimate these two variables. With this estimate of $\mathrm{E}[\max_k\{\widehat{\mathrm{SR}}_k\}]$, we can test whether $\max_k\{\widehat{\mathrm{SR}}_k\}$ is statistically significant, using the deflated Sharpe ratio (Bailey and López de Prado 2014).

The second approach estimates the number of trials, K, and applies Šidàk's correction to derive the familywise error rate (FWER). The FWER provides an adjusted rejection threshold on which we can test whether $\max_k\{\widehat{SR_k}\}$ is statistically significant, using the distributions proposed by Lo (2002) and Mertens (2002). Researchers can use these analytical estimates of the familywise false positives probability and familywise false negatives probability when they design their statistical tests.

8.10 Exercises

1 Following the approach described in Section 8.2, plot the precision and recall associated with a test as a function of $\theta \in [0, 1]$, where $\alpha = \beta = 0.05$ and $K = 1$. Is this consistent with your intuition?
2 Repeat Exercise 1, plotting a surface as a function of $K = 1, \ldots, 25$. What is the overall effect of multiple testing on precision and recall?
3 Consider a strategy with five years of daily IID Normal returns. The best trial out of ten yields an annualized Sharpe ratio of 2, where the variance across the annualized Sharpe ratios is 1.
   a What is the expected maximum Sharpe ratio? Hint: Apply the False Strategy theorem.
   b After one trial, what is the probability of observing a maximum Sharpe ratio equal or higher than 2? Hint: This is the probabilistic Sharpe ratio.
   c After ten trials, what is the probability of observing a maximum Sharpe ratio equal or higher than 2? Hint: This is the deflated Sharpe ratio.
4 Consider an investment strategy that buys S&P 500 futures when a price moving average with a short lookback exceeds a price moving average with a longer lookback.
   a Generate 1,000 times series of strategy returns by applying different combinations of
      i Short lookback
      ii Long lookback
      iii Stop-loss
      iv Profit taking
      v Maximum holding period
   b Compute the maximum Sharpe ratio out of the 1,000 experiments.
   c Derive $E[\max_k\{\widehat{SR_k}\}]$, as explained in Section 8.7.
   d Compute the probability of observing a Sharpe ratio equal to or higher than 4(b).
5 Repeat Exercise 4, where this time you compute the familywise Type I and Type II errors, where SR^* is the median across the 1,000 Sharpe ratios.

Appendix A: Testing on Synthetic Data

Synthetic data sets allow researchers to test investment strategies on series equivalent to thousands of historical years, and prevent overfitting to a particular observed data set. Generally speaking, these synthetic data sets can be generated via two approaches: resampling and Monte Carlo. Figure A.1 summarizes how these approaches branch out and relate to each other.

Resampling consists of generating new (unobserved) data sets by sampling repeatedly on the observed data set. Resampling can be deterministic or random. Instances of deterministic resampling include jackknife (leave-one-out), cross-validation (one-fold-out), and combinatorial cross-validation (permutation tests). For instance, one could divide the historical observations into N folds and compute all testing sets that result from leaving k folds out. This combinatorial cross-validation yields $\frac{k}{N}\binom{N}{N-k}$ complete historical paths, which are harder to overfit than a single-path historical backtest (see AFML, chapter 12, for an implementation). Instances of random resampling include subsampling (random sampling without replacement) and bootstrap (random sampling with replacement). Subsampling relies on weaker assumptions, however it is impractical when the observed data set has limited size. Bootstrap can generate samples as large as the observed data set, by drawing individual observations or blocks of them (hence preserving the serial dependence of the observations). The effectiveness of a bootstrap depends on the independence of the random samples, a requirement inherited from the central limit theorem. To make the random draws as independent as possible, the sequential bootstrap adjusts online the probability of drawing observations similar to those already sampled (see AFML, chapter 4, for an implementation).

The second approach to generating synthetic data sets is Monte Carlo. A Monte Carlo randomly samples new (unobserved) data sets from an estimated population or data-generating process, rather than from an observed data set (like a bootstrap would do). Monte Carlo experiments can be parametric or nonparametric. An instance of a parametric Monte Carlo is a regime-switching time series model (Hamilton 1994), where samples are drawn from alternative processes, $n = 1, \ldots, N$, and where the probability $p_{t,n}$ of drawing from process n at time t is a function of the process from which the previous observation was drawn (a Markov chain). Expectation-maximization algorithms can be used to estimate the probability of transitioning from one process to another at time t (the transition probability matrix). This parametric approach allows researchers to match the statistical properties of the observed data set, which are then

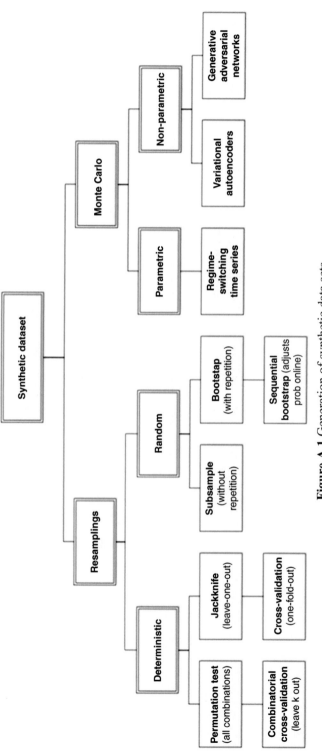

Figure A.1 Generation of synthetic data sets.

replicated in the unobserved data set. One caveat of parametric Monte Carlo is that the data-generating process may be more complex than a finite set of algebraic functions can replicate. When that is the case, nonparametric Monte Carlo experiments may be of help, such as variational autoencoders, self-organizing maps, or generative adversarial networks. These methods can be understood as nonparametric, nonlinear estimators of latent variables (similar to a nonlinear PCA). An autoencoder is a neural network that learns how to represent high-dimensional observations in a low-dimensional space. Variational auto-encoders have an additional property which makes their latent spaces continuous. This allows for successful random sampling and interpolation and, in turn, their use as a generative model. Once a variational autoencoder has learned the fundamental structure of the data, it can generate new observations that resemble the statistical properties of the original sample, within a given dispersion (hence the notion of "variational"). A self-organizing map differs from auto-encoders in that it applies competitive learning (rather than error-correction), and it uses a neighborhood function to preserve the topological properties of the input space. Generative adversarial networks train two competing neural networks, where one network (called a generator) is tasked with generating simulated observations from a distribution function, and the other network (called a discriminator) is tasked with predicting the probability that the simulated observations are false given the true observed data. The two neural networks compete with each other, until they converge to an equilibrium. The original sample on which the nonparametric Monte Carlo is trained must be representative enough to learn the general characteristics of the data-generating process, otherwise a parametric Monte Carlo approach should be preferred (see AFML, chapter 13, for an example).

Appendix B: Proof of the "False Strategy" Theorem

It is known that the maximum value in a sample of independent random variables following an exponential distribution converges asymptotically to a Gumbel distribution. For a proof, see Embrechts et al. (2003, 138–47). As a particular case, the Gumbel distribution covers the Maximum Domain of Attraction of the Gaussian distribution, and therefore it can be used to estimate the expected value of the maximum of several independent random Gaussian variables.

To see how, suppose a sample of independent and identically distributed Gaussian random variables, $y_k \sim \mathcal{N}[0, 1], k = 1, \ldots, K$. If we apply the Fisher–Tippet–Gnedenko theorem to the Gaussian distribution, we derive an approximation for the sample maximum, $\max_k \{y_k\}$, leading to

$$\lim_{K \to \infty} \text{prob} \left[\frac{\max_k \{y_k\} - \alpha}{\beta} \leq x \right] = G[x], \tag{1}$$

where $G[x] = e^{-e^{-x}}$ is the CDF for the Standard Gumbel distribution, $\alpha = Z^{-1}[1 - (1/K)]$, $\beta = Z^{-1}[1 - (1/K)e^{-1}] - \alpha$, and Z^{-1} corresponds to the inverse of the Standard Normal's CDF. See Resnick (1987) and Embrechts et al. (2003) for a derivation of the normalizing constants (α, β).

The limit of the expectation of the normalized maxima from a distribution in the Gumbel Maximum Domain of Attraction (see Proposition 2.1(iii) in Resnick 1987) is

$$\lim_{K \to \infty} E \left[\frac{\max_k \{y_k\} - \alpha}{\beta} \right] = \gamma, \tag{2}$$

where γ is the Euler–Mascheroni constant, $\gamma \approx 0.5772 \ldots$ For a sufficiently large K, the mean of the sample maximum of standard normally distributed random variables can be approximated by

$$E[\max_k \{y_k\}] \approx \alpha + \gamma\beta = (1 - \gamma)Z^{-1}\left[1 - \frac{1}{K}\right] + \gamma Z^{-1}\left[1 - \frac{1}{K}e^{-1}\right], \tag{3}$$

where $K \pounds 1$.

Now consider a set of estimated performance statistics $\{\widehat{SR}_k\}, k = 1, \ldots, K$, with independent and identically distributed Gaussian $\widehat{SR}_k \sim \mathcal{N}[0, V[\{\widehat{SR}_k\}]]$.

We make use of the linearity of the expectation operator, to derive the expression

$$E[\max_k\{\widehat{SR}_k\}]\left(V[\{\widehat{SR}_k\}]\right)^{-1/2} \approx (1-\gamma)Z^{-1}\left[1-\frac{1}{K}\right] + \gamma Z^{-1}\left[1-\frac{1}{Ke}\right].$$

(4)

This concludes the proof of the theorem.

Bibliography

Aggarwal, C., and C. Reddy (2014): *Data Clustering – Algorithms and Applications*. 1st ed. CRC Press.

Ahmed, N., A. Atiya, N. Gayar, and H. El-Shishiny (2010): "An Empirical Comparison of Machine Learning Models for Time Series Forecasting." *Econometric Reviews*, Vol. 29, No. 5–6, pp. 594–621.

Anderson, G., A. Guionnet, and O. Zeitouni (2009): *An Introduction to Random Matrix Theory*. 1st ed. Cambridge Studies in Advanced Mathematics. Cambridge University Press.

Ballings, M., D. van den Poel, N. Hespeels, and R. Gryp (2015): "Evaluating Multiple Classifiers for Stock Price Direction Prediction." *Expert Systems with Applications*, Vol. 42, No. 20, pp. 7046–56.

Bansal, N., A. Blum, and S. Chawla (2004): "Correlation Clustering." *Machine Learning*, Vol. 56, No. 1, pp. 89–113.

Benjamini, Y., and D. Yekutieli (2001): "The Control of the False Discovery Rate in Multiple Testing under Dependency." *Annals of Statistics*, Vol. 29, pp. 1165–88.

Benjamini, Y., and W. Liu (1999): "A Step-Down Multiple Hypotheses Testing Procedure that Controls the False Discovery Rate under Independence." *Journal of Statistical Planning and Inference*, Vol. 82, pp. 163–70.

Benjamini, Y., and Y. Hochberg (1995): "Controlling the False Discovery Rate: A Practical and Powerful Approach to Multiple Testing." *Journal of the Royal Statistical Society*, Series B, Vol. 57, pp. 289–300.

Bontempi, G., S. Taieb, and Y. Le Borgne (2012): "Machine Learning Strategies for Time Series Forecasting." *Lecture Notes in Business Information Processing*, Vol. 138, No. 1, pp. 62–77.

Booth, A., E. Gerding, and F. McGroarty (2014): "Automated Trading with Performance Weighted Random Forests and Seasonality." *Expert Systems with Applications*, Vol. 41, No. 8, pp. 3651–61.

Cao, L., and F. Tay (2001): "Financial Forecasting Using Support Vector Machines." *Neural Computing and Applications*, Vol. 10, No. 2, pp. 184–92.

Cao, L., F. Tay, and F. Hock (2003): "Support Vector Machine with Adaptive Parameters in Financial Time Series Forecasting." *IEEE Transactions on Neural Networks*, Vol. 14, No. 6, pp. 1506–18.

Cervello-Royo, R., F. Guijarro, and K. Michniuk (2015): "Stockmarket Trading Rule Based on Pattern Recognition and Technical Analysis: Forecasting the

DJIA Index with Intraday Data." *Expert Systems with Applications*, Vol. 42, No. 14, pp. 5963–75.

Chang, P., C. Fan, and J. Lin (2011): "Trend Discovery in Financial Time Series Data Using a Case-Based Fuzzy Decision Tree." *Expert Systems with Applications*, Vol. 38, No. 5, pp. 6070–80.

Chen, B., and J. Pearl (2013): "Regression and Causation: A Critical Examination of Six Econometrics Textbooks." *Real-World Economics Review*, Vol. 65, pp. 2–20.

Creamer, G., and Y. Freund (2007): "A Boosting Approach for Automated Trading." *Journal of Trading*, Vol. 2, No. 3, pp. 84–96.

Creamer, G., and Y. Freund (2010): "Automated Trading with Boosting and Expert Weighting." *Quantitative Finance*, Vol. 10, No. 4, pp. 401–20.

Creamer, G., Y. Ren, Y. Sakamoto, and J. Nickerson (2016): "A Textual Analysis Algorithm for the Equity Market: The European Case." *Journal of Investing*, Vol. 25, No. 3, pp. 105–16.

Dixon, M., D. Klabjan, and J. Bang (2017): "Classification-Based Financial Markets Prediction Using Deep Neural Networks." *Algorithmic Finance*, Vol. 6, No. 3, pp. 67–77.

Dunis, C., and M. Williams (2002): "Modelling and Trading the Euro/US Dollar Exchange Rate: Do Neural Network Models Perform Better?" *Journal of Derivatives and Hedge Funds*, Vol. 8, No. 3, pp. 211–39.

Easley, D., and J. Kleinberg (2010): *Networks, Crowds, and Markets: Reasoning about a Highly Connected World*. 1st ed. Cambridge University Press.

Easley, D., M. López de Prado, M. O'Hara, and Z. Zhang (2011): "Microstructure in the Machine Age." Working paper.

Efroymson, M. (1960): "Multiple Regression Analysis." In A. Ralston and H. Wilf (eds.), *Mathematical Methods for Digital Computers*. 1st ed. Wiley.

Einav, L., and J. Levin (2014): "Economics in the Age of Big Data." *Science*, Vol. 346, No. 6210. Available at http://science.sciencemag.org/content/346/6210/1243089

Feuerriegel, S., and H. Prendinger (2016): "News-Based Trading Strategies." *Decision Support Systems*, Vol. 90, pp. 65–74.

Greene, W. (2012): *Econometric Analysis*. 7th ed. Pearson Education.

Harvey, C., and Y. Liu (2015): "Backtesting." *The Journal of Portfolio Management*, Vol. 42, No. 1, pp. 13–28.

Harvey, C., and Y. Liu (2018): "False (and Missed) Discoveries in Financial Economics." Working paper. Available at https://ssrn.com/abstract=3073799

Harvey, C., and Y. Liu (2018): "Lucky Factors." Working paper. Available at https://ssrn.com/abstract=2528780

Hastie, T., R. Tibshirani, and J. Friedman (2016): *The Elements of Statistical Learning: Data Mining, Inference and Prediction*. 2nd ed. Springer.

Bibliography

Hayashi, F. (2000): *Econometrics*. 1st ed. Princeton University Press.

Holm, S. (1979): "A Simple Sequentially Rejective Multiple Test Procedure." *Scandinavian Journal of Statistics*, Vol. 6, pp. 65–70.

Hsu, S., J. Hsieh, T. Chih, and K. Hsu (2009): "A Two-Stage Architecture for Stock Price Forecasting by Integrating Self-Organizing Map and Support Vector Regression." *Expert Systems with Applications*, Vol. 36, No. 4, pp. 7947–51.

Huang, W., Y. Nakamori, and S. Wang (2005): "Forecasting Stock Market Movement Direction with Support Vector Machine." *Computers and Operations Research*, Vol. 32, No. 10, pp. 2513–22.

Ioannidis, J. (2005): "Why Most Published Research Findings Are False." *PLoS Medicine*, Vol. 2, No. 8. Available at https://doi.org/10.1371/journal.pmed.0020124

James, G., D. Witten, T. Hastie, and R. Tibshirani (2013): *An Introduction to Statistical Learning*. 1st ed. Springer.

Kahn, R. (2018): *The Future of Investment Management*. 1st ed. CFA Institute Research Foundation.

Kara, Y., M. Boyacioglu, and O. Baykan (2011): "Predicting Direction of Stock Price Index Movement Using Artificial Neural Networks and Support Vector Machines: The Sample of the Istanbul Stock Exchange." *Expert Systems with Applications*, Vol. 38, No. 5, pp. 5311–19.

Kim, K. (2003): "Financial Time Series Forecasting Using Support Vector Machines." *Neurocomputing*, Vol. 55, No. 1, pp. 307–19.

Kolanovic, M., and R. Krishnamachari (2017): "Big Data and AI Strategies: Machine Learning and Alternative Data Approach to Investing." *J.P. Morgan Quantitative and Derivative Strategy*, May.

Kolm, P., R. Tutuncu, and F. Fabozzi (2010): "60 Years of Portfolio Optimization." *European Journal of Operational Research*, Vol. 234, No. 2, pp. 356–71.

Krauss, C., X. Do, and N. Huck (2017): "Deep Neural Networks, Gradient-Boosted Trees, Random Forests: Statistical Arbitrage on the S&P 500." *European Journal of Operational Research*, Vol. 259, No. 2, pp. 689–702.

Kuan, C., and L. Tung (1995): "Forecasting Exchange Rates Using Feedforward and Recurrent Neural Networks." *Journal of Applied Econometrics*, Vol. 10, No. 4, pp. 347–64.

Kuhn, H. W., and A. W. Tucker (1952): "Nonlinear Programming." In *Proceedings of 2nd Berkeley Symposium*. University of California Press, pp. 481–92.

Laborda, R., and J. Laborda (2017): "Can Tree-Structured Classifiers Add Value to the Investor?" *Finance Research Letters*, Vol. 22, pp. 211–26.

López de Prado, M. (2018): "A Practical Solution to the Multiple-Testing Crisis in Financial Research." *Journal of Financial Data Science*, Vol. 1, No. 1. Available at https://ssrn.com/abstract=3177057

López de Prado, M., and M. Lewis (2018): "Confidence and Power of the Sharpe Ratio under Multiple Testing." Working paper. Available at https://ssrn.com/abstract=3193697

MacKay, D. (2003): *Information Theory, Inference, and Learning Algorithms.* 1st ed. Cambridge University Press.

Marcenko, V., and L. Pastur (1967): "Distribution of Eigenvalues for Some Sets of Random Matrices." *Matematicheskii Sbornik*, Vol. 72, No. 4, pp. 507–36.

Michaud, R. (1998): *Efficient Asset Allocation: A Practical Guide to Stock Portfolio Optimization and Asset Allocation.* Boston: Harvard Business School Press.

Nakamura, E. (2005): "Inflation Forecasting Using a Neural Network." *Economics Letters*, Vol. 86, No. 3, pp. 373–78.

Olson, D., and C. Mossman (2003): "Neural Network Forecasts of Canadian Stock Returns Using Accounting Ratios." *International Journal of Forecasting*, Vol. 19, No. 3, pp. 453–65.

Otto, M. (2016): *Chemometrics: Statistics and Computer Application in Analytical Chemistry.* 3rd ed. Wiley.

Patel, J., S. Sha, P. Thakkar, and K. Kotecha (2015): "Predicting Stock and Stock Price Index Movement Using Trend Deterministic Data Preparation and Machine Learning Techniques." *Expert Systems with Applications*, Vol. 42, No. 1, pp. 259–68.

Pearl, J. (2009): "Causal Inference in Statistics: An Overview." *Statistics Surveys*, Vol. 3, pp. 96–146.

Plerou, V., P. Gopikrishnan, B. Rosenow, L. Nunes Amaral, and H. Stanley (1999): "Universal and Nonuniversal Properties of Cross Correlations in Financial Time Series." *Physical Review Letters*, Vol. 83, No. 7, pp. 1471–74.

Porter, K. (2017): "Estimating Statistical Power When Using Multiple Testing Procedures." Available at www.mdrc.org/sites/default/files/PowerMultiplicity-IssueFocus.pdf

Potter, M., J. P. Bouchaud, and L. Laloux (2005): "Financial Applications of Random Matrix Theory: Old Laces and New Pieces." *Acta Physica Polonica B*, Vol. 36, No. 9, pp. 2767–84.

Qin, Q., Q. Wang, J. Li, and S. Shuzhi (2013): "Linear and Nonlinear Trading Models with Gradient Boosted Random Forests and Application to Singapore Stock Market." *Journal of Intelligent Learning Systems and Applications*, Vol. 5, No. 1, pp. 1–10.

Robert, C. (2014): "On the Jeffreys–Lindley Paradox." *Philosophy of Science*, Vol. 81, No. 2, pp. 216–32.

Shafer, G. (1982): "Lindley's Paradox." *Journal of the American Statistical Association*, Vol. 77, No. 378, pp. 325–34.

Simon, H. (1962): "The Architecture of Complexity." *Proceedings of the American Philosophical Society*, Vol. 106, No. 6, pp. 467–82.

SINTEF (2013): "Big Data, for Better or Worse: 90% of World's Data Generated over Last Two Years." *Science Daily*, May 22. Available at www.sciencedaily.com/releases/2013/05/130522085217.htm

Sorensen, E., K. Miller, and C. Ooi (2000): "The Decision Tree Approach to Stock Selection." *Journal of Portfolio Management*, Vol. 27, No. 1, pp. 42–52.

Theofilatos, K., S. Likothanassis, and A. Karathanasopoulos (2012): "Modeling and Trading the EUR/USD Exchange Rate Using Machine Learning Techniques." *Engineering, Technology and Applied Science Research*, Vol. 2, No. 5, pp. 269–72.

Trafalis, T., and H. Ince (2000): "Support Vector Machine for Regression and Applications to Financial Forecasting." *Neural Networks*, Vol. 6, No. 1, pp. 348–53.

Trippi, R., and D. DeSieno (1992): "Trading Equity Index Futures with a Neural Network." *Journal of Portfolio Management*, Vol. 19, No. 1, pp. 27–33.

Tsai, C., and S. Wang (2009): "Stock Price Forecasting by Hybrid Machine Learning Techniques." *Proceedings of the International Multi-Conference of Engineers and Computer Scientists*, Vol. 1, No. 1, pp. 755–60.

Tsai, C., Y. Lin, D. Yen, and Y. Chen (2011): "Predicting Stock Returns by Classifier Ensembles." *Applied Soft Computing*, Vol. 11, No. 2, pp. 2452–59.

Tsay, R. (2013): *Multivariate Time Series Analysis: With R and Financial Applications*. 1st ed. Wiley.

Wang, J., and S. Chan (2006): "Stock Market Trading Rule Discovery Using Two-Layer Bias Decision Tree." *Expert Systems with Applications*, Vol. 30, No. 4, pp. 605–11.

Wang, Q., J. Li, Q. Qin, and S. Ge (2011): "Linear, Adaptive and Nonlinear Trading Models for Singapore Stock Market with Random Forests." In *Proceedings of the 9th IEEE International Conference on Control and Automation*, pp. 726–31.

Wei, P., and N. Wang (2016): "Wikipedia and Stock Return: Wikipedia Usage Pattern Helps to Predict the Individual Stock Movement." In *Proceedings of the 25th International Conference Companion on World Wide Web*, Vol. 1, pp. 591–94.

Wooldridge, J. (2010): *Econometric Analysis of Cross Section and Panel Data*. 2nd ed. MIT Press.

Wright, S. (1921): "Correlation and Causation." *Journal of Agricultural Research*, Vol. 20, pp. 557–85.

Żbikowski, K. (2015): "Using Volume Weighted Support Vector Machines with Walk Forward Testing and Feature Selection for the Purpose of Creating Stock Trading Strategy." *Expert Systems with Applications*, Vol. 42, No. 4, pp. 1797–1805.

Zhang, G., B. Patuwo, and M. Hu (1998): "Forecasting with Artificial Neural Networks: The State of the Art." *International Journal of Forecasting*, Vol. 14, No. 1, pp. 35–62.

Zhu, M., D. Philpotts, and M. Stevenson (2012): "The Benefits of Tree-Based Models for Stock Selection." *Journal of Asset Management*, Vol. 13, No. 6, pp. 437–48.

Zhu, M., D. Philpotts, R. Sparks, and J. Stevenson (2011): "A Hybrid Approach to Combining CART and Logistic Regression for Stock Ranking." *Journal of Portfolio Management*, Vol. 38, No. 1, pp. 100–109.

References

American Statistical Association (2016): "Statement on Statistical Significance and P-Values." Available at www.amstat.org/asa/files/pdfs/P-ValueStatement .pdf

Apley, D. (2016): "Visualizing the Effects of Predictor Variables in Black Box Supervised Learning Models." Available at https://arxiv.org/abs/ 1612.08468

Athey, Susan (2015): "Machine Learning and Causal Inference for Policy Evaluation." In *Proceedings of the 21st ACM SIGKDD International Conference on Knowledge Discovery and Data Mining*, pp. 5–6. ACM.

Bailey, D., and M. López de Prado (2012): "The Sharpe Ratio Efficient Frontier." *Journal of Risk*, Vol. 15, No. 2, pp. 3–44.

Bailey, D., and M. López de Prado (2013): "An Open-Source Implementation of the Critical-Line Algorithm for Portfolio Optimization." *Algorithms*, Vol. 6, No. 1, pp. 169–96. Available at http://ssrn.com/abstract=2197616

Bailey, D., and M. López de Prado (2014): "The Deflated Sharpe Ratio: Correcting for Selection Bias, Backtest Overfitting and Non-Normality." *Journal of Portfolio Management*, Vol. 40, No. 5, pp. 94–107.

Bailey, D., J. Borwein, M. López de Prado, and J. Zhu (2014): "Pseudo-mathematics and Financial Charlatanism: The Effects of Backtest Overfitting on Out-of-Sample Performance." *Notices of the American Mathematical Society*, Vol. 61, No. 5, pp. 458–71. Available at http://ssrn .com/abstract=2308659

Black, F., and R. Litterman (1991): "Asset Allocation Combining Investor Views with Market Equilibrium." *Journal of Fixed Income*, Vol. 1, No. 2, pp. 7–18.

Black, F., and R. Litterman (1992): "Global Portfolio Optimization." *Financial Analysts Journal*, Vol. 48, No. 5, pp. 28–43.

Breiman, L. (2001): "Random Forests." *Machine Learning*, Vol. 45, No. 1, pp. 5–32.

Brian, E., and M. Jaisson (2007): "Physico-theology and Mathematics (1710–1794)." In *The Descent of Human Sex Ratio at Birth*. Springer Science & Business Media, pp. 1–25.

Brooks, C., and H. Kat (2002): "The Statistical Properties of Hedge Fund Index Returns and Their Implications for Investors." *Journal of Alternative Investments*, Vol. 5, No. 2, pp. 26–44.

Cavallo, A., and R. Rigobon (2016): "The Billion Prices Project: Using Online Prices for Measurement and Research." NBER Working Paper 22111, March.

CFTC (2010): "Findings Regarding the Market Events of May 6, 2010." *Report of the Staffs of the CFTC and SEC to the Joint Advisory Committee on Emerging Regulatory Issues*, September 30.

Christie, S. (2005): "Is the Sharpe Ratio Useful in Asset Allocation?" MAFC Research Paper 31. Applied Finance Centre, Macquarie University.

Clarke, Kevin A. (2005): "The Phantom Menace: Omitted Variable Bias in Econometric Research." *Conflict Management and Peace Science*, Vol. 22, No. 1, pp. 341–52.

Clarke, R., H. De Silva, and S. Thorley (2002): "Portfolio Constraints and the Fundamental Law of Active Management." *Financial Analysts Journal*, Vol. 58, pp. 48–66.

Cohen, L., and A. Frazzini (2008): "Economic Links and Predictable Returns." *Journal of Finance*, Vol. 63, No. 4, pp. 1977–2011.

De Miguel, V., L. Garlappi, and R. Uppal (2009): "Optimal versus Naive Diversification: How Inefficient Is the 1/N Portfolio Strategy?" *Review of Financial Studies*, Vol. 22, pp. 1915–53.

Ding, C., and X. He (2004): "K-Means Clustering via Principal Component Analysis." In *Proceedings of the 21st International Conference on Machine Learning*. Available at http://ranger.uta.edu/~chqding/papers/KmeansPCA1.pdf

Easley, D., M. López de Prado, and M. O'Hara (2011a): "Flow Toxicity and Liquidity in a High-Frequency World." *Review of Financial Studies*, Vol. 25, No. 5, pp. 1457–93.

Easley, D., M. López de Prado, and M. O'Hara (2011b): "The Microstructure of the 'Flash Crash': Flow Toxicity, Liquidity Crashes and the Probability of Informed Trading." *Journal of Portfolio Management*, Vol. 37, No. 2, pp. 118–28.

Efron, B., and T. Hastie (2016): *Computer Age Statistical Inference: Algorithms, Evidence, and Data Science*. 1st ed. Cambridge University Press.

Embrechts, P., C. Klueppelberg, and T. Mikosch (2003): *Modelling Extremal Events*. 1st ed. Springer.

Goutte, C., P. Toft, E. Rostrup, F. Nielsen, and L. Hansen (1999): "On Clustering fMRI Time Series." *NeuroImage*, Vol. 9, No. 3, pp. 298–310.

Grinold, R., and R. Kahn (1999): *Active Portfolio Management*. 2nd ed. McGraw-Hill.

Gryak, J., R. Haralick, and D. Kahrobaei (Forthcoming): "Solving the Conjugacy Decision Problem via Machine Learning." *Experimental Mathematics*. Available at https://doi.org/10.1080/10586458.2018.1434704

Hacine-Gharbi, A., and P. Ravier (2018): "A Binning Formula of Bi-histogram for Joint Entropy Estimation Using Mean Square Error Minimization." *Pattern Recognition Letters*, Vol. 101, pp. 21–28.

Hacine-Gharbi, A., P. Ravier, R. Harba, and T. Mohamadi (2012): "Low Bias Histogram-Based Estimation of Mutual Information for Feature Selection." *Pattern Recognition Letters*, Vol. 33, pp. 1302–8.

Hamilton, J. (1994): *Time Series Analysis*. 1st ed. Princeton University Press.

Harvey, C., Y. Liu, and C. Zhu (2016): ". . . and the Cross-Section of Expected Returns." *Review of Financial Studies*, Vol. 29, No. 1, pp. 5–68. Available at https://ssrn.com/abstract=2249314

Hodge, V., and J. Austin (2004): "A Survey of Outlier Detection Methodologies." *Artificial Intelligence Review*, Vol. 22, No. 2, pp. 85–126.

IDC (2014): "The Digital Universe of Opportunities: Rich Data and the Increasing Value of the Internet of Things." *EMC Digital Universe with Research and Analysis*. April. Available at www.emc.com/leadership/digital-universe/2014iview/index.htm

Ingersoll, J., M. Spiegel, W. Goetzmann, and I. Welch (2007): "Portfolio Performance Manipulation and Manipulation-Proof Performance Measures." *The Review of Financial Studies*, Vol. 20, No. 5, pp. 1504–46.

Jaynes, E. (2003): *Probability Theory: The Logic of Science*. 1st ed. Cambridge University Press.

Jolliffe, I. (2002): *Principal Component Analysis*. 2nd ed. Springer.

Kraskov, A., H. Stoegbauer, and P. Grassberger (2008): "Estimating Mutual Information." Working paper. Available at https://arxiv.org/abs/cond-mat/0305641v1

Laloux, L., P. Cizeau, J. P. Bouchaud, and M. Potters (2000): "Random Matrix Theory and Financial Correlations." *International Journal of Theoretical and Applied Finance*, Vol. 3, No. 3, pp. 391–97.

Ledoit, O., and M. Wolf (2004): "A Well-Conditioned Estimator for Large-Dimensional Covariance Matrices." *Journal of Multivariate Analysis*, Vol. 88, No. 2, pp. 365–411.

Lewandowski, D., D. Kurowicka, and H. Joe (2009): "Generating Random Correlation Matrices Based on Vines and Extended Onion Method." *Journal of Multivariate Analysis*, Vol. 100, pp. 1989–2001.

Liu, Y. (2004): "A Comparative Study on Feature Selection Methods for Drug Discovery." *Journal of Chemical Information and Modeling*, Vol. 44, No. 5, pp. 1823–28. Available at https://pubs.acs.org/doi/abs/10.1021/ci049875d

Lo, A. (2002): "The Statistics of Sharpe Ratios." *Financial Analysts Journal*, July, pp. 36–52.

Lochner, M., J. McEwen, H. Peiris, O. Lahav, and M. Winter (2016): "Photometric Supernova Classification with Machine Learning." *The Astrophysical Journal*, Vol. 225, No. 2. Available at http://iopscience.iop .org/article/10.3847/0067-0049/225/2/31/meta

López de Prado, M. (2016): "Building Diversified Portfolios that Outperform Out-of-Sample." *Journal of Portfolio Management*, Vol. 42, No. 4, pp. 59–69.

López de Prado, M. (2018a): *Advances in Financial Machine Learning*. 1st ed. Wiley.

López de Prado, M. (2018b): "The 10 Reasons Most Machine Learning Funds Fail." *The Journal of Portfolio Management*, Vol. 44, No. 6, pp. 120–33.

López de Prado, M. (2019a): "A Data Science Solution to the Multiple-Testing Crisis in Financial Research." *Journal of Financial Data Science*, Vol. 1, No. 1, pp. 99–110.

López de Prado, M. (2019b): "Beyond Econometrics: A Roadmap towards Financial Machine Learning." Working paper. Available at https://ssrn .com/abstract=3365282

López de Prado, M. (2019c): "Ten Applications of Financial Machine Learning." Working paper. Available at https://ssrn.com/abstract=3365271

López de Prado, M., and M. Lewis (2018): "Detection of False Investment Strategies Using Unsupervised Learning Methods." Working paper. Available at https://ssrn.com/abstract=3167017

Louppe, G., L. Wehenkel, A. Sutera, and P. Geurts (2013): "Understanding Variable Importances in Forests of Randomized Trees." In *Proceedings of the 26th International Conference on Neural Information Processing Systems*, pp. 431–39.

Markowitz, H. (1952): "Portfolio Selection." *Journal of Finance*, Vol. 7, pp. 77–91.

Meila, M. (2007): "Comparing Clusterings – an Information Based Distance." *Journal of Multivariate Analysis*, Vol. 98, pp. 873–95.

Mertens, E. (2002): "Variance of the IID estimator in Lo (2002)." Working paper, University of Basel.

Molnar, C. (2019): "Interpretable Machine Learning: A Guide for Making Black-Box Models Explainable." Available at https://christophm.github .io/interpretable-ml-book/

Mullainathan, S., and J. Spiess (2017): "Machine Learning: An Applied Econometric Approach." *Journal of Economic Perspectives*, Vol. 31, No. 2, pp. 87–106.

Neyman, J., and E. Pearson (1933): "IX. On the Problem of the Most Efficient Tests of Statistical Hypotheses." *Philosophical Transactions of the Royal Society, Series A*, Vol. 231, No. 694–706, pp. 289–337.

Opdyke, J. (2007): "Comparing Sharpe Ratios: So Where Are the p-Values?" *Journal of Asset Management*, Vol. 8, No. 5, pp. 308–36.

Parzen, E. (1962): "On Estimation of a Probability Density Function and Mode." *The Annals of Mathematical Statistics*, Vol. 33, No. 3, pp. 1065–76.

Resnick, S. (1987): *Extreme Values, Regular Variation and Point Processes*. 1st ed. Springer.

Romer, P. (2016): "The Trouble with Macroeconomics." *The American Economist*, September 14.

Rosenblatt, M. (1956): "Remarks on Some Nonparametric Estimates of a Density Function." *The Annals of Mathematical Statistics*, Vol. 27, No. 3, pp. 832–37.

Rousseeuw, P. (1987): "Silhouettes: A Graphical Aid to the Interpretation and Validation of Cluster Analysis." *Computational and Applied Mathematics*, Vol. 20, pp. 53–65.

Schlecht, J., M. Kaplan, K. Barnard, T. Karafet, M. Hammer, and N. Merchant (2008): "Machine-Learning Approaches for Classifying Haplogroup from Y Chromosome STR Data." *PLOS Computational Biology*, Vol. 4, No. 6. Available at https://doi.org/10.1371/journal.pcbi.1000093

Sharpe, W. (1966): "Mutual Fund Performance." *Journal of Business*, Vol. 39, No. 1, pp. 119–38.

Sharpe, W. (1975): "Adjusting for Risk in Portfolio Performance Measurement." *Journal of Portfolio Management*, Vol. 1, No. 2, pp. 29–34.

Sharpe, W. (1994): "The Sharpe Ratio." *Journal of Portfolio Management*, Vol. 21, No. 1, pp. 49–58.

Šidàk, Z. (1967): "Rectangular Confidence Regions for the Means of Multivariate Normal Distributions." *Journal of the American Statistical Association*, Vol. 62, No. 318, pp. 626–33.

Solow, R. (2010): "Building a Science of Economics for the Real World." Prepared statement of Robert Solow, Professor Emeritus, MIT, to the House Committee on Science and Technology, Subcommittee on Investigations and Oversight, July 20.

Steinbach, M., E. Levent, and V. Kumar (2004): "The Challenges of Clustering High Dimensional Data." In L. Wille (ed.), *New Directions in Statistical Physics*. 1st ed. Springer, pp. 273–309.

Štrumbelj, E., and I. Kononenko (2014): "Explaining Prediction Models and Individual Predictions with Feature Contributions." *Knowledge and Information Systems*, Vol. 41, No. 3, pp. 647–65.

Varian, H. (2014): "Big Data: New Tricks for Econometrics." *Journal of Economic Perspectives*, Vol. 28, No. 2, pp. 3–28.

Wasserstein, R., A. Schirm, and N. Lazar (2019): "Moving to a World beyond p<0.05." *The American Statistician*, Vol. 73, No. 1, pp. 1–19.

Wasserstein, R., and N. Lazar (2016): "The ASA's Statement on p-Values: Context, Process, and Purpose." *The American Statistician*, Vol. 70, pp. 129–33.

Witten, D., A. Shojaie, and F. Zhang (2013): "The Cluster Elastic Net for High-Dimensional Regression with Unknown Variable Grouping." *Technometrics*, Vol. 56, No. 1, pp. 112–22.

Acknowledgments

Professor Riccardo Rebonato kindly invited me to publish this Element in the series he edits for *Cambridge Elements in Quantitative Finance*. Professor Frank Fabozzi made substantive suggestions regarding the Element's content and scope. Many of the techniques introduced in this Element were tested in the course of my work at Lawrence Berkeley National Laboratory, for which I am particularly grateful to Professor Horst Simon and Dr. Kesheng Wu. Finally, I wish to recognize my approximately thirty coauthors for the past twenty years, for their enduring support and inspiration.

About the Author

Marcos M. López de Prado is a professor of practice at Cornell University's School of Engineering, and the CIO of True Positive Technologies (TPT). Dr. López de Prado has over 20 years of experience developing investment strategies with the help of machine learning algorithms and supercomputers. In 2019, he received the 'Quant of the Year Award' from *The Journal of Portfolio Management*. For more information, visit www.QuantResearch.org

Cambridge Elements ☰

Quantitative Finance

Riccardo Rebonato

EDHEC Business School

Editor Riccardo Rebonato is Professor of Finance at EDHEC Business School and holds the PIMCO Research Chair for the EDHEC Risk Institute. He has previously held academic positions at Imperial College, London, and Oxford University and has been Global Head of Fixed Income and FX Analytics at PIMCO, and Head of Research, Risk Management and Derivatives Trading at several major international banks. He has previously been on the Board of Directors for ISDA and GARP, and he is currently on the Board of the Nine Dot Prize. He is the author of several books and articles in finance and risk management, including *Bond Pricing and Yield Curve Modelling* (2017, Cambridge University Press).

About the Series

Cambridge *Elements in Quantitative Finance* aims for broad coverage of all major topics within the field. Written at a level appropriate for advanced undergraduate or graduate students and practitioners, *Elements* combines reports on original research covering an author's personal area of expertise, tutorials and masterclasses on emerging methodologies, and reviews of the most important literature.

Cambridge Elements ≡

Quantitative Finance

Made in the USA
Coppell, TX
26 November 2020